Take Charge

Using Everyday
Canadian English

Take Charge
Using Everyday Canadian English

Lucia Pietrusiak Engkent

Prentice Hall Allyn & Bacon Canada Inc., Scarborough, Ontario

Canadian Cataloguing in Publication Data

Engkent, Lucia Pietrusiak, 1955-
    Take charge: using everyday Canadian English

ISBN 0-13-185653-7

1. English language -- Textbooks for second language learners.*
2. English language -- Spoken English -- Canada.
3. Canadianisms (English).*   I. Title.

PE1128.E525 1997   428.3'4   C96-931865-0

 © 1997 Prentice-Hall Canada Inc.,
Scarborough, Ontario
A Division of Simon & Schuster/A Viacom Company

Allyn and Bacon, Inc., Needham Heights, MA
Prentice-Hall, Inc., Columbus, Ohio
Prentice-Hall, Inc., Upper Saddle River, New Jersey
Prentice-Hall International (UK) Limited, London
Prentice-Hall of Australia, Pty. Limited, Sydney
Prentice-Hall Hispanoamericana, S.A., Mexico City
Prentice-Hall of India Private Limited, New Delhi
Prentice-Hall of Japan, Inc., Tokyo
Simon & Schuster Asia Private Limited, Singapore
Editora Prentice-Hall do Brasil, Ltda., Rio de Janeiro

ISBN 0-13-185653-7

Acquisitions Editor: D. Roberge
Developmental Editor: M. Tomins
Copy Editor: J. Sweet
Production Editor: M. Farahbaksh
Production Coordinator: J. Schell
Cover Image: D. Gauthier
Page Layout: J. Morrison

2 3 4 5   BBG   01 00 99 98

Printed and bound in the United States of America

Every reasonable effort has been made to obtain permissions for
all articles and data used in this edition. If errors or omissions have
occurred, they will be corrected in future editions provided written
notification has been received by the publisher.

We welcome readers' comments, which can be sent by e-mail to
    phabinfo_pubcanada@prenhall.com

Table of Contents

Introduction

Themes

This text is thematically arranged, with material divided into six units showing a different setting—school, the community, the mall, work, home, and the road. Various topics and issues are explored in each unit. For example, "In the Community" discusses facilities such as libraries and recreation centres as well as issues related to being a neighbour. "On the Road" focuses on transportation, travel, and tourism.

The topics have been chosen to introduce a broad range of subjects and issues within the setting.

The main focus of the text is everyday life in Canada. The language of the dialogues is everyday Canadian English—its idioms, shortened forms, and common expressions. The information notes give information about Canadian life and culture.

Level

The material is designed for students with an intermediate level of competence in English. It is assumed that students have a basic knowledge of grammatical structure and vocabulary. The prose passages and the speech in the dialogues are not in simplified English.

Students learning a second language bring a range of abilities and experiences to class. For instance, if they have learned English "on the streets," their knowledge is much different from that of people who studied English in a classroom in their own country.

This range of ability and knowledge should be capitalized on. For example, computer-literate students can practise their speaking skills by explaining computers to their classmates and teaching the vocabulary of computers. People who have recently learned to drive can share their experience and knowledge with others.

Organization

The text is designed to allow teachers and students to pick and choose the material of interest to them. It is not necessary to work through the book sequentially.

Some sections in each unit apply to the general theme of the unit; other sections are linked to dialogues within the unit. For example, "An Apple for the Teacher" relates back to the setting of the unit—the school. However, a section such as "Talking about Your Aches and Pains" expands on the examples found in the dialogue "Calling in Sick." The grammar sections usually take up a point presented in one of the dialogues.

Information Notes

The prose passages are designed to give information about Canadian life and culture, to give students a chance to learn and practise vocabulary, to give background information for the dialogues, and to serve as a starting point for class discussion. These texts are not presented as reading exercises, although some have comprehension questions.

Dialogues

The dialogues illustrate one aspect of the topic and present a slice of Canadian life. As well as serving as a springboard for discussion, these dialogues provide a context for idioms and expressions and illustrate features of spoken Canadian English.

The language in the dialogues is not simplified English. Instead, they are kept short enough that intermediate students can cope with them.

Words and Phrases

Throughout the text, key words and expressions are printed in boldface type. Students can learn the meaning of the vocabulary in several ways: from the context, by using a dictionary, in class discussion, and through the exercises.

Different exercises are provided to help students learn the vocabulary. Some require students to match words with definitions. Some are fill-in-the-blank sentences or paragraphs. Some are questions designed to encourage students to build on the knowledge they have, to use reference materials, and to think about the vocabulary item and related words and expressions.

Follow-up

Dialogues and prose passages are followed by different types of questions. Some of these questions focus on comprehension; they require students to find main ideas and retell the story. Other questions ask students to relate their own experiences to the topic of the reading or the dialogue. Students should be given the opportunity to steer the discussion to the topics that interest them most.

Grammar

Take Charge is not a grammar text. Sections on grammar explain structures that have come up in a dialogue. For example, "To Suppose" further explores the use of **suppose**, from the dialogue "An Overnight Visit."

Teachers may have to supplement these sections on grammar, if students are unaware of the terminology or if they lack basic information about English grammar.

Assignments

Assignments extend the topics discussed in the classroom into real-life situations. Some of these involve field trips, such as a visit to a grocery store. Others require the students to make phone calls to find information. And still others bring material from everyday life into the classroom for examination.

The assignments are deliberately open-ended. This method allows the teacher to tailor the assignments to the particular class and to give specific instructions as needed. Teachers can also distribute assignments among students. For example, instead of having every student in the class call the Ministry of Transportation to find out about driving regulations, the teacher can assign a few students to this task and assign different students to the next similar assignment.

Assignments should be discussed in class. Students may have questions concerning vocabulary or suggestions concerning the assignment.

At the end of each unit is a section called "More to Do," which suggests assignments related to the theme of the unit. These are usually more ambitious than assignments found in the body of the unit. They can be done as class projects or can be broken up into individual tasks. Teachers can tailor the tasks to the students and specify exactly how the assignment will be carried out.

Writing Exercises

Although this book does not teach writing skills, students have an opportunity to practise these skills in each unit. The writing assignments are not academic essays; rather, they mirror real-life writing situations, such as writing a note to a teacher or a complaint letter to a business. For additional writing practice, discussion questions can be used as essay topics.

Answer Key

The answers to the grammar and vocabulary exercises are found in the back of the text.

Instructor's Manual

An instructor's manual is available. It offers suggestions for teachers and provides supplementary exercises, including games and puzzles.

Audio Cassette

The audio cassette gives the students the opportunity to hear the dialogues spoken by native speakers of Canadian English.

Acknowledgments

I am grateful to the many people who have contributed to this publication. I appreciate the hard work by the staff of Prentice Hall, especially Marta Tomins, who was there to listen to me and push me when I needed it. Thank you to the reviewers who offered helpful comments on the earlier versions of this work: Manuela Gobbato, LINC, North York Board of Education; Patricia Parsons, Seneca College; and Avril Taylor, Mohawk College.

Most of all, I am thankful for the support of my family. My husband, Garry, provided valuable input and reviewed every word I wrote.

AT SCHOOL

SCHOOLING IN CANADA

Education is a provincial responsibility, but schools are administered by local **school boards**.

Kindergarten is for children who are four or five years old. Children begin formal full-day **schooling** in Grade 1, when they are about six years old. They must stay in school **at least** until they are sixteen. However, most students continue to finish high school. Some go on to college or university.

Each year of schooling represents one grade. (The school year extends from the beginning of September to the end of June.) **Elementary** school includes kindergarten to about Grade 8. **Secondary** school (or high school) may start in Grade 8, 9, or 10 and it usually continues until Grade 12.

In Canada, students may go to university or to a community college. If they want to learn skills for a specific job, they attend college for one to four years to get a **diploma** or **certificate.** For example, lab technicians, child-care workers, and hotel managers go to college. Universities offer **degree** programs as well as training in certain **professions**, such as law, medicine, and teaching.

Universities offer three main levels of **degrees.** Students earn a **bachelor's degree** after three or four years of study. A **master's degree** can take another year or two. A **doctorate** may take a further three to seven years to complete.

SCHOOLS IN YOUR NATIVE COUNTRY

Answer these questions about schools in your native country:

1. What kind of administration does the school system have?
2. How old are children when they begin school?
3. How are the levels of schooling divided?
4. What kind of education is available for high school graduates?
5. How many years of study are required for university degrees?

Follow-up

1. In small groups, discuss the Canadian school system. Tell about your experiences. What do you know about Canadian schools from friends and relatives?

2. Make a list of the elementary and secondary schools in your neighbourhood. You can use a city map and a phone book to help you.
3. Look at calendars from local colleges and universities. Compare the programs offered at the different types of school. Calendars can be found in the library.

STARTING SCHOOL

Secretary:	May I help you?
Parent:	Yes, we just moved to the area and I'd like to **register** my daughter for school.
Secretary:	How old is she?
Parent:	She just **turned** five last month.
Secretary:	Then she can start kindergarten in September. Here is our kindergarten registration package. It includes information **pamphlets** and registration forms. Did you bring your child's birth certificate?
Parent:	No, I didn't.
Secretary:	We'll need to see it to register her. And this form has to be signed by your doctor saying that your child has had her **shots.**
Parent:	OK, that shouldn't be a problem.

Secretary: Why don't you take this home and **look it over**? When you've **filled in** the forms, come back with the necessary **documents**, and we'll do the registration. Is that all right?

Parent: That's fine. Thank you.

Secretary: You can give me a call if you have any questions. The number's in here.

Words and phrases

1. What does "She just **turned** five" mean?

2. Several types of medication are given by **injection**. Some are **immunizations** or **vaccinations** that prevent diseases such as measles or polio. School children are required to have several **vaccinations**. Informally, people say they are going to have their **shots** or they are going to get a **needle**.

   We're getting a new dog, but it's just a puppy and it hasn't had all its **shots** yet.

   I had to get some more **shots** before my trip to Africa.

   He's afraid of **needles**.

Contact your public health department to get information about vaccinations.

Follow-up

1. Does the parent register his child for school in the dialogue? Explain what happens and what the parent must do next.

2. What are the documents that the parent must bring in?

3. Find out about school registration for children in a local school. What documents does the school want to see?

REGISTRATION REQUIREMENTS

Use the words in the list to fill in the blanks in the paragraphs that follow.

calendar

counsellors

evaluate

fill out

placement test

prerequisite

tuition

Registering for school may require several steps. First, you choose your program by looking in the school _____ . This booklet gives course descriptions, timetables, and other important information.

Sometimes _____ help you choose your courses. You may have to meet certain conditions to take a course. For example, some classes may have _____ courses, such as introductory courses. Sometimes special arrangements have to be made, and you must get the professor's permission. For courses that require a certain level of skill, such as language classes, you may have to write a _____ before registering. These tests help teachers _____ your level.

When you choose your courses, you also _____ a registration form and pay _____ fees.

SIGNING UP FOR AN ENGLISH COURSE

Mrs. Lau: May I help you?

Alina: Yes, please. I'd like to **sign up** for an English course.

Mrs. Lau: What kind of course are you interested in?

Alina: Um, I don't know. I'd like to improve

my writing—for reports and letters at work.

Mrs. Lau: Have you read this **brochure**? It describes the courses we offer. We have beginner, intermediate and advanced levels, and we have specialized writing courses, such as business and technical writing.

Alina: **I looked through** the brochure, but I'm not sure which course is right for me.

Mrs. Lau: If you haven't taken a class here before, you could take the **placement test** we have for the writing courses.

Alina: OK. That sounds like a good idea.

Mrs. Lau: Here is a list of essay topics. Pick one and write a couple of paragraphs. Take half an hour **or so.** When you finish writing your essay, bring it back here and we'll **evaluate** it and suggest a course to **suit** you.

Alina: All right. Thank you.

Words and phrases

Look at this pair of sentences. Do they mean the same thing? What is the difference between **register** and **sign up**?

> I'm going to register for a course in Japanese flower arrangement.

> I'm going to sign up for a course in Japanese flower arrangement.

Here are some other examples of how these words are used:

> If you are already a student here, you can **register** for this course by phone.

> When you check into a hotel, you sign the guest **register.**

> I'm looking for the **registration** desk.

> I'd like to **sign up** for the soccer program.

> She passed around a **sign-up** sheet so she could check the attendance.

Follow-up

1. What does Alina have to do before she registers for a writing course?

2. How do you think Alina's writing will be evaluated? What will the teacher look for?

3. Have you ever written a placement test? What did you think of the test?

4. Discuss registration at your school. Is it a simple procedure? How could it be improved?

SCHOOL CALENDARS

Bring a school brochure or calendar to class. You can choose a calendar from a college, a university, or a continuing education department in your local school board. In small groups, look at the calendars and discuss them.

What information is given in the publication?

- course descriptions
- dates and times for courses
- course fees
- a registration form
- pictures
- a campus map

Is the publication attractive?

Is it easy to read?

Does it give enough information?

Does it have a table of contents or an index?

If you have different publications, decide which one is the most effective.

SPENDING TIME ON TIME

In the dialogue "Signing up for an English Course," the teacher tells the student to "take half an hour" to write the essay. Many different verbs can be used with the word **time**, or with quantities of time, such as hours or days. These verbs include:

> find, give, have, keep, kill, lose, make, pass, spare, spend, take, waste

Usually the meaning of the expression is clear. Using the verbs correctly is more difficult than understanding them.

For the following sentences, use the verbs listed above to fill in the blanks. (Not all the verbs in the list are used, and more than one verb may fit the sentence.) Use the correct form of the verb to fit the tense in the sentence. Discuss the answers in class to make sure you understand each expression.

1. Do you _____ a minute? I'd like to talk to you now.

2. I've never really _____ any time with her, so I don't know her very well.

3. _____ your time. You don't have to rush.

4. _____ me a minute. I'm not ready yet.

5. This watch doesn't _____ good time. I'm often late for my appointments.

6. We walked around the mall because we had some time to _____ before the movie started.

7. Janice says she's very busy, but I think that if she really wanted to see us, she'd _____ time.

8. I don't really like to _____ any more time on housework than the absolute minimum.

9. I have to hurry. I don't have a second to _____.

10. Time seems to _____ so slowly when I'm in class.

PHRASAL VERBS

Phrasal verbs are very common in informal spoken English. In the dialogues, for example, the speakers say "sign up" rather than "enrol" or "register." All three verbs have the same meaning, but the phrasal verb is less formal.

A **phrasal verb** is more than one word—in other words, a **phrase.** Phrasal verbs are also called "two-word" or "two-part" verbs; some are "three-word" verbs.

Phrasal verbs are made of a verb with one or two **particles.** Phrasal verbs are usually with short, common verbs such as **be, come, make,** and **give.**

Phrasal verbs are confusing for non-native speakers to learn, especially since some are idioms. However, they are an important feature of spoken English.

Here are some hints for learning phrasal verbs:

- Pay attention to phrasal verbs when you hear or read them. Make sure you understand what they mean.

- Phrasal verbs are more common in spoken English and in informal written English. More formal, single verbs are used in writing.

  The teacher **gave out** the textbooks.

  The teacher **distributed** the textbooks.

- Learn the meaning of the whole expression—the verb with the particle. A different particle can change the whole meaning of the verb.

  I need to clean the cupboards, but I keep **putting** it **off**. (delaying)

  Put my name **down** for Saturday's trip. (record, enter)

- Be aware that some phrasal verbs have more than one meaning.

  I didn't get a chance to **bring up** the issue at the meeting. (mention)

  His parents **brought** him **up** to be totally honest. (raised)

- Learn the grammatical structure that each phrasal verb requires.

  Some phrasal verbs have objects.

  Emilio **turned on** the television.

  Emilio **turned** the television **on**.

  Some phrasal verbs cannot be separated (that is, the object cannot be placed between the verb and the adverb). These are usually three-part verbs and two-word verbs ending in **about**, **across**, **against**, or **into**.

  I'll **look into** the matter, *not* I'll look the matter into

  I can't **come up with** a topic for this essay.

- Look for patterns. Sometimes a particle will have a similar meaning with several verbs. For example, the particle **up** sometimes gives the meaning that an action is done "completely."

  I tore the paper into two pieces.

  I **tore up** the paper. (into small pieces)

  The children ate their vegetables.

  The children **ate up** their vegetables.

Rewrite the following paragraph by inserting the phrasal verbs in the blanks. You may have to change the tense and the word order.

blow up

break down

call off

get up

leave behind

look forward to

pick up

put out

take down

I had a bad day at school. It got off to a bad start when I _____ late. I'd been _____ the field trip that was planned, but then I discovered that the bus had _____ and the field trip _____ . So we ended up having the regular schedule and I hadn't done my math homework. I even _____ my notebook _____ and I had to _____ my notes on a scrap piece of paper. Then, in chemistry lab, my Bunsen burner _____ . Luckily, no one was close by at the time and the teacher _____ the fire _____ quickly. My brother had promised to give me a ride home, but he forgot to _____ and I had to take the bus.

Did you find two phrasal verbs in the paragraph above? Study these expressions and other phrasal verbs you hear or read.

SLANG

Generally, spoken English is less formal than written English. Spoken English has words and phrases that may not be correct to use in formal writing. In dictionaries, these terms are marked **informal** or **colloquial** English. A third word that has the same meaning is **conversational** English.

Another kind of language, which is *very* informal, is **slang**. Slang, however, is less acceptable than colloquial English in formal speech and writing. Moreover, slang may vary from place to place and it changes over time. For example, something that was very good was called "groovy" in the 1960s and "radical" in the 1980s. Both words sound odd today.

The dividing line between slang and informal English is not distinct. Sometimes words start out as slang, spread in use, and become part of everyday informal English. For instance, calling children "kids" has become so common that the word is now considered informal English rather than slang.

Use a dictionary to find out whether the following words are considered informal or slang:

buck (dollar)

cool (very good)

dough (money)

drag (boring person or situation)

jock (male who plays in a lot of sports)

wimp (a weak person)

Slang expressions are fun to learn, even if they cannot be used in all situations. Teenagers often have their own slang expressions, and some of these describe school situations. For example, a course that is very easy and that is not taken seriously might be called "a Mickey Mouse course" or "a bird course."

Speak to some Canadian high school, college, and university students. Ask them to tell you their slang terms for school situations. You may find slang expressions to describe:

- a student who always gets high marks
- a student who is always trying to get the teacher's attention
- a course that is very easy and not taken seriously
- a difficult course
- staying up all night to study
- missing class deliberately
- a teacher who is very strict, or one who is not strict
- cheating on a test
- first-year students
- study period, time off class
- different kinds of students (e.g. athletic students)
- studying for an exam at the last minute

AN APPLE FOR THE TEACHER

Teachers, schools, and students are symbolized by different pictures. For example, obvious items such as blackboards and chalk are used to represent school. Students are also shown by the symbols of graduation—rolled-up diplomas, graduation gowns, and mortarboards (squared hats with tassels).

Apples also serve as a symbol. Traditionally, a shiny, red apple was a common gift for a teacher. Now, even though the custom no longer exists, apples remain associated with teachers.

THE LEARNING EXPERIENCE

Going into a new class is always an adventure for students. Even when they are familiar with the school or the subject, a new course usually means a new teacher, and every teacher has a different way of doing things. Students must **get used to** the class expectations, which vary from teacher to teacher, school to school, and culture to culture.

Some classrooms have a quiet, controlled atmosphere; students raise their hands and wait to be called upon to speak. Other teachers encourage a more casual environment; students work individually and in groups, and exchange ideas. Generally, Canadian teachers think that students who are active participants learn more than those who are passive listeners.

Going to university or college after high school is a big change for students. They are treated as adults, responsible for their own education. They do not receive as much guidance from their parents or teachers. In fact, many students find they cannot **cope**. The **drop-out** rate for first-year students is high.

What was the biggest change you experienced in your education? How did you adjust to the change?

THEIR FIRST UNIVERSITY LECTURE

Maria: **Whew**, we survived—our first class.

Zach: That wasn't a class, that was a **zoo**. Are all our lectures **gonna** be like that?

Maria: I hope not. What do you **figure**—maybe 600 **kids** in that lecture hall?

Zach: At least.

Lynn: Well, hey, it's better than Alison's **psych** course. They watch their professor's lectures on videotape.

Maria: What if they have questions?

Lynn: There's a **T.A.** in the class to answer them.

Zach: **Geez.**

Words and phrases

1. Match the shortened form with the correct long form.

    gonna   go to

                    going to

                    go not

    psych   psychiatry

                    psychology

                    psychosomatic

    T.A.   talent agent

                    transportation associate

                    teaching assistant

    geez   gee whiz

                    go please

                    gee it's

2. Why did Zach call the class a **zoo**?

Follow-up

1. What do Zach and Maria think of their first class?

2. How is Alison's course different?

3. Have you had overcrowded or very large classes? Tell about your experience.

SCHOOL DAYS STORIES

Outside class, talk to your friends and relatives about their school experiences. Ask them about the kinds

cuss the advantages and disadvantages of the strategies. Which are the best strategies?

1. Bring a tape recorder to class. Listen to the lecture again and again at home.

2. Take a secretarial **shorthand** course and try to take down every word the professor says.

3. Make sure you are prepared for the lectures by doing the readings in advance.

4. Develop your own abbreviations and learn to write very quickly.

5. Concentrate on understanding the lecture and take down the important ideas in point form.

USED TO

Used to appears in two common expressions in English, with different verb forms and different meanings. Look at the difference in these two sentences:

a) Elaine **used to** drive long distances a lot.

b) Elaine is **used to** driving long distances.

Discuss the difference in meaning.

Here are some example sentences. In small groups, discuss the meaning of each sentence.

1. She used to be very outgoing when she was younger, but now she's very quiet.

2. I don't mind cleaning out the change rooms. I'm used to it by now.

3. I used to enjoy skating, but now I find it hurts my feet too much.

4. I'm used to his practical jokes, so I know what to expect.

5. They used to go to that school before they moved.

6. He's used to the noise of the train and doesn't even notice it.

Write five sentences using "used to." Show the two different grammatical structures and meanings in your sentences.

WISE WORDS

Many proverbs are about learning and school. What do these sayings mean to you? Do you agree with the idea?

---

of rules and teachers they had in school. Pick the most interesting story you hear and tell it to the class.

Here are some examples of stories about school:

"My friend told me about a professor she had who didn't lecture—he just read aloud from the course textbook. If a student asked the professor to explain something, he would just read that part of the textbook again."

"My aunt told me that she had to wear school uniforms and that there were strict rules about clothing. (This was in the days of miniskirts.) The teachers would make the girls kneel on the floor—the hem of the skirt had to touch the floor."

NOTE-TAKING

First-year university students often find it difficult to learn to take notes in lectures. High school teachers often write a lot on the blackboard. University professors use **overhead projectors** and give out **handouts,** but students are expected to make notes as they listen to the lecture.

Here are some **strategies** (ways, techniques) for dealing with note-taking in lectures. In groups, dis-

A little learning is a dangerous thing.

Practise what you preach.

Learn to walk before you run.

You can't teach an old dog new tricks.

MEET THE TEACHER

Parents talk to their child's teacher in different situations. A "Meet the Teacher" **open house** is an informal get-together at the beginning of the school year. After report cards are sent home, parents may have a scheduled interview with the teacher. In addition, teachers often phone parents if they see a problem developing with a student. Parents can also arrange to talk to the teacher whenever they want to discuss their child's school work.

During interview evenings, time is often a problem. Appointments are short, and parents have to wait their turn. Therefore, it is important to arrive and leave **on time.** Parents can bring a list of questions or points to discuss with the teacher. If they **run out of time,** another interview can be scheduled to continue the discussion.

What are the different situations where parents and teachers communicate? Which four are mentioned above?

A PARENT–TEACHER INTERVIEW

Mrs. Shigeta: Mr. and Mrs. Carter? So nice to see you again. Please come in and **have a seat.**

Mr. Carter: Thank you.

Mrs. Shigeta: You'll be pleased to hear that Emma has been doing very well in school this term. She is playing more with the other children and not just watching them **from the sidelines.**

Mrs. Carter: That's good. I've noticed that she talks more about her friends in school now. She is quite shy, and she felt **uneasy** about starting in a new school.

Mrs. Shigeta: Well, she's **settled in** very well. **Academically,** you don't have to worry about her. Her reading is **above grade level** and she has a good understanding of the math we've been doing.

Mr. Carter: We just got a new computer game that helps children with their math and Emma has started playing with that.

Mrs. Shigeta: That's good as long as she enjoys it, but I don't think you need to push her too much. She's a good student and it's important that she continues to enjoy learning.

Words and phrases

1. What are other ways of saying **have a seat**?
2. Give synonyms for **uneasy**.
3. Explain what is meant by **above grade level**.

At a school open house, parents meet the teachers and look at displays in the classrooms. Usually, these events last only one or two hours, so visitors should arrive on time.

People have open-house parties where their home is open to their friends for several hours. The friends drop by for a short visit during that time. This kind of party is especially common around Christmas.

A real-estate open house allows interested buyers to drop in to look at a house without making an appointment.

In small groups, discuss the kinds of open-house events you have attended. Write a sample invitation for an open house at your school or for a party at your home.

REPORT CARD COMMENTS

Most report cards include comments from teachers as well as the grades. These are carefully worded because teachers try to avoid saying very negative things about a student's work.

Here are some sample comments. In small groups, discuss each phrase. Do you understand what the teacher is saying? Is the comment favourable or not? Can you think of other ways to say the same thing?

- has the potential for much better work
- excellent achievement
- assignments and homework frequently incomplete
- good effort
- participates enthusiastically
- doing satisfactory work
- must assume more personal responsibility for learning
- although progress is slow, a good effort has been made
- an improvement in attitude is expected
- grasps theoretical concepts, has difficulty with practical application
- shows a keen interest in this subject
- needs to make better use of class time
- a pleasure to have in the class

Follow-up

1. What problem did Emma have at the beginning of the school year? Why? How is this problem being solved? Do you think this problem is serious?

2. What does the teacher think of Emma's school work?

3. What advice does the teacher give at the end of the interview? What do you think of this advice?

4. How can parents help their children to do well at school?

OPEN HOUSES

Generally, the term **open house** is used for "drop-in" social or business events. Guests are expected to make a brief visit sometime during the hours of the open house. However, a business open house may have a program for which guests are expected to arrive and leave at scheduled times.

NOTES TO THE TEACHER

Parents often have to send notes to their children's teachers. These notes may explain an absence from class or lateness.

April 22, 1995

Dear Mrs. Lum,

Natasha will have to leave school early on Thursday because she has a doctor's appointment downtown. I will come to pick her up at 2:00. I hope that this will not be **inconvenient**.

Mike Polanski

E-mail has become a popular way for college and university students to communicate with professors.

```
To:       timlin@uofx.ca (Prof. Mark Timlin)
From:     hazar@uofx.ca (Alisha Hazar)
Date:     96.11.24 11:07 a.m.
Subject:  unable to write midterm
```

A family emergency has come up and I have to leave town immediately. I will not be able to write the **midterm** test which is scheduled for tomorrow. I'm sorry that I was unable to reach you by phone today. I hope that I can make arrangements for a **make-up** test when I return to class.

Words and phrases

1. What is the opposite of **inconvenient**? Is **inconvenient** a noun, verb, adjective, or adverb? What is the noun form?

2. Define these different kinds of exams and tests:

   midterm test

   make-up test

   final exam

   open-book exam

   pop quiz

Follow-up

1. Why did Mike Polanski send a note to the teacher? Summarize the message in your own words.

2. Why did Alisha Hazar send a note to her professor? Summarize the message in your own words.

3. What expressions are used in the notes to make them polite?

4. Have you had to write similar notes? In what situations? Discuss.

Write it out

Write a note to a teacher for one of the following situations:

as a parent:

- your child was absent from school the previous day;

- you wish to make an appointment to see your child's teacher;

- your child will be absent for a few days and you want homework to be sent home with the child's brother or sister.

as a student:

- you need an **extension** (more time) for an assignment;

- you would like a letter of reference from your professor;

- you are having trouble with an assignment and would like to see the professor, but you cannot come during regular office hours.

MORE TO DO

1. Write a paragraph on one of the following topics:

- what makes a good teacher

- how to be a successful student

- a comparison of a class in Canada and one in your native country

- why education is important

- the best way to learn a second language

2. Interview a teacher or a school official about his or her job. Give an oral report or write a written report about the interview. Before your interview, be sure to make a list of questions.

3. In small groups, write a brochure to advertise your school or class. Or, make a video advertisement—a commercial.

4. With your class, write a report (or make a video documentary) on "The Life of a Foreign Student."

In the Community

LIVING IN A COMMUNITY

Canadians have many kinds of services and facilities in their communities. For example, local government may operate libraries or recreation centres, which are funded by taxes and cost little for residents to use. Facilities include swimming pools, skating rinks, tennis courts, and gymnasiums. Programs and lessons are offered to both children and adults.

In addition to government-run programs, people organize clubs and special-interest groups in their community. There may be singing clubs, neighbourhood watch programs, and community theatre.

Joining such clubs and using local facilities are good ways to meet other people living in the community. This approach is especially important since today's lifestyles can make it difficult to get to know your neighbours. For instance, because many people spend long hours working far from home, they do not have as many opportunities to talk to their friends and neighbours.

However, Canadian society may see more socialization among neighbours in the future. More people are choosing lifestyles that keep them home more often. For example, many people run home-based businesses. When people know their neighbours, they have a stronger community spirit and their neighbourhoods are safer and better places to live.

Follow-up

1. Do you like your neighbourhood? Would you be willing to move to another area?

2. How well do you know your neighbours? Why is it harder to get to know neighbours today than it used to be?

3. What are some good ways to meet people living in your neighbourhood?

4. Why is it good to live in a neighbourhood where people know each other?

5. How could home offices improve community life?

ASK THE LIBRARIAN

Librarian: Good morning. May I help you?

Patron 1: Yes, please. I'm looking for some information on CompuWorks. I have a job interview with them next week and I'd like to know more about the company.

Librarian: Certainly. We have **annual reports** from many local companies on the shelf at the far right. They are in alphabetical order by company name. And here is a **directory** of local businesses, which gives basic information on different companies. If you can't find what you need there, come back and I'll see if I can find you anything else.

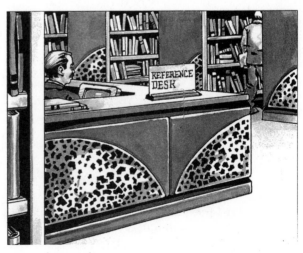

Patron 1:   Great. Thank you very much.

Patron 2:   Excuse me. I'm looking for a novel called *The Stone Angel,* but I can't remember the author's name.

Librarian: You can find books listed by title in our catalogue. Have you used our computer catalogue before?

Patron 2:   No, I'm not very good with this **high-tech** stuff.

Librarian: This catalogue is pretty easy to use. Here, I'll show you. This is the opening **menu.** You want to search for a book by its title, so you choose number 1 from the list on the screen.

Patron 2:   That looks easy enough.

Librarian: Now you type in the title, like this— the stone angel. You don't even have to bother with capital letters.

Patron 2:   Great.

Librarian: And here's a list of books with your title or a similar one. This might be your book—it's by Margaret Laurence.

Patron 2:   That's right. I remember her name now.

Librarian: You'll find it in the fiction section over there. The books are in alphabetical order by author.

Patron 2:   Thank you very much. And I think I can use the computer **by myself** next time.

Librarian: If you have any problems, don't hesitate to ask.

Patron 3:   Excuse me, I was wondering how to get a library card.

Librarian: Are you a resident of Maplewood?

Patron 3:   Yes.

Librarian: Here's a form for you to fill out. We'll need some identification with your address to prove you are a **resident.**

Patron 3:   And how much does it cost?

Librarian: Your card is free, but if you lose it, a replacement card costs $2. This pamphlet will explain the Maplewood library system. If you have any other questions, you can ask here or at the **circulation desk.**

Patron 3:   Thank you.

Words and phrases

1. What is the purpose of an **annual report**?
2. Describe a **directory.** Give an example.
3. What is the long form of **high tech**? What is the opposite? Give examples of both.
4. What are the similarities and differences between restaurant menus and computer menus?

Follow-up

1. Why is the first patron looking for information on CompuWorks? What kind of information would it be useful for a job applicant to know?
2. Why did Patron 2 not look in the library catalogue?
3. Computer catalogues have replaced card catalogues. Which do you prefer? Why?
4. Why does the librarian ask Patron 3 whether he is a resident of the city?
5. Are public libraries a good use of government money? What do you think libraries will be like in the future?

LIBRARY WORDS AND EXPRESSIONS

Here is a list of important words and expressions that you might use in a library. Use words from the list to fill in the blanks in the passage below.

bar code

borrow

call number

catalogue

circulation

due date

look up

overdue

reference

When you need to find a book in the library, you consult the _____ . Books are listed by author, title, and subject. Libraries may record their books on cards, in microfilm records, or in computers.

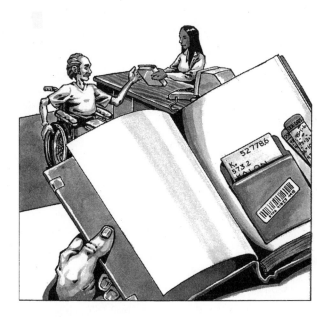

When you find the record of the book you want, it is important to take a note of the _____ , which is a series of numbers and letters that tells you where the book is on the shelves.

If you need help finding the information you need, you ask the librarian at the _____ desk.

Some books in the library do not **circulate** (you cannot borrow them). These books are reference books such as dictionaries and encyclopedias. You can use them in the library to _____ the information you need.

After you have selected the books you wish to borrow, you take them to the _____ desk. If the library is computerized, the librarian uses a scanner to read the _____ on your library card and on each of the books.

When you _____ books, you should check the _____ to know when you have to return the books. You have to pay **fines** on _____ (late) books.

A VISIT TO THE PUBLIC LIBRARY

Visit your local public library or a school library. You may be able to arrange a guided tour for the class, or you can visit the library on your own. Plan your trip by making a list of questions. Some of the questions will be answered in signs and brochures. For other questions, you might have to ask a librarian.

Here are some questions you might ask on your visit:

Who can get a library card? How do you get a library card?

Which books cannot be taken out of the library?

What is the **circulation period** for books? (In other words, how long can you keep them?)

Can you reserve a book? Can you order a book from another library?

What kind of catalogues (computer, card, microfilm) does the library have? Practise using the catalogue.

Find out what types of materials your library has, such as:

- music cassettes or compact disks
- videotapes
- magazines and newspapers (periodicals)
- books and tapes in other languages
- large print books
- books read aloud on cassette tapes (audio books)
- CD-ROMs (reference material on computer disk)
- simplified books for adults learning to read or learning English

What kinds of activities and programs take place in the library? For example, some libraries have reading clubs and story times for children.

CHECK IT OUT

Fill in the blanks in the sentences with either **check in** or **check out**.

1.   _____ time in the hotel is 11 a.m., so make sure you get everything packed up early.

2.   The airline recommends getting to the airport an hour before the flight so that you have time to _____.

3.   The _____ lines at the supermarket are always very long.

4.   She'll be going to the University of Waterloo in the fall, so she's gone down to _____ the campus, the residences, and the city.

5.   _____ it _____! I just bought this new CD.

SWIMMING LESSONS

Clerk 1:   **Parks and Rec.** May I help you?

Gerald: Yes, hello. I'd like some information about your adult swim classes.

Clerk 1:   Just a moment, sir. I'll connect you with our **aquatics** division.

Clerk 2:   Aquatics.

Gerald: Yes. I have some questions about the adult swim classes.

Clerk 2:   Certainly, sir. What would you like to know?

Gerald: I see in your **brochure** that you have different levels of adult classes. Do you have a course for adults with a fear of the water?

Clerk 2:   Yes. The first-level class is designed specifically for adults who are uncomfortable in the water.

Gerald: So, you have lots of people with that problem?

Clerk 2:   Quite a few. We have a special program. Our instructors go slowly, first getting each student **used to** putting **their** head under water.

Gerald: Sounds good. Do I register at my local pool?

Clerk 2:   Yes, and you can talk to the instructor there if you want more details about the program.

Gerald: Thank you very much.

Words and phrases

1. **Aquatics** is a broad term for water sports. What sports could be included?

2. **Rec** is an informal shortened form. What is the full form of the word?

3. Note that **their** is a plural pronoun, used in the dialogue with the singular noun "each student." This is actually ungrammatical, but it is common in everyday speech because it is awkward to say "his or her." "Their" as a singular pronoun meaning "his or her" is becoming increasingly acceptable, even in writing.

Follow-up

1. Why does Gerald speak to two clerks in the Parks and Recreation Department?

2. Notice what the clerks say when they answer the phone. How are business calls answered differently from calls to a home?

3. What does Gerald want to know? What information does he have already?

4. Does Gerald find the clerk's information reassuring? Explain.

5. Have you ever taken swimming lessons? Tell your classmates about your experience.

6. People who are afraid of water may have had a frightening experience, perhaps almost drowning. Have you ever had a bad experience in the water?

7. Have you ever tried to **get over** (or **overcome**) a fear?

8. Do you think swimming is a good recreational activity? Discuss the advantages and disadvantages.

CALL THE REC CENTRE

Pick up a brochure for recreational services in your area. In small groups, discuss the programs and facilities available. Make a list of questions that may not be answered in the brochure. For example:

Can people have their skates sharpened at the arena? How much does it cost?

Is there a seniors' club or a youth drop-in centre at the recreation centre? What kind of activities does the centre have?

What kind of martial arts are taught: judo, karate, tae kwon do? What are the qualifications of the instructors?

What life-saving procedures are taught in the children's swim classes?

In pairs, role-play making phone calls to find out more information about the recreation programs.

Be sure to start with a short, general question or statement, so that you can make sure you are connected to the right person before you start on a detailed explanation.

From your practice questions, choose one program that interests you and make an actual call to the recreation centre from home. Report to the class on the information you received.

FEARS

Some of the common words for fear are found in the sample sentences below. For each sentence, identify the word in bold as a **noun**, a **verb**, or an **adjective**. Look at the sentence structure that is used with the word.

1. He's **frightened** of the dark.

    He's **scared** of the dark.

    He's **afraid** of the dark.

2. The loud noise **scared** the baby.

    The loud noise **frightened** the baby.

3. I have a **fear** of failure.

4. She **fears** that she won't be able to meet the deadline.

    She is **afraid** that she won't be able to meet the deadline.

5. That picture certainly gave him a **fright**.

6. Those movie monsters were certainly **scary**.

Those movie monsters were certainly **frightening**.

Write other example sentences to show how these words are used. Make sure you understand the different sentence patterns shown here. For example, a person **fears** something, but something **frightens** a person.

The words **terror**, **terrify**, **terrifying**, and **terrified** are used for a very intense (strong) fear. Substitute the forms of **terrify** in the sentences above to form grammatical sentences.

Tell your classmates about a frightening experience you have had.

CHILDREN'S LESSONS

Canadian parents seem to spend much of their time as **chauffeurs**, driving their children to school, lessons, and various other activities. This is a fairly recent change in lifestyle. Before, children had more free time, they played with friends in their neighbourhood, and they used bicycles to get around. Now, parents worry about their children being out by themselves.

Children often participate in a wide range of lessons and activities after school and on weekends. They might take music lessons or dance classes or play in hockey or soccer **leagues**.

The popularity of such activities is another demand on families' free time. Sometimes, children's lessons provide a rare opportunity for their parents to socialize with other parents. They talk with one another as they wait in the pool gallery, in **the stands** at the rink, or at the door of the gym or dance studio.

HE SHOOTS! HE SCORES?

Parent 1:	He's got a **breakaway**!
Parent 2:	What? Who?
Parent 3:	Go, Jason, go!
Parent 1:	**Deke** him! Deke him!
Parent 2:	There's the shot!
Parent 3:	Did it go in?
Parent 2:	No. Great **save**!
Parent 1:	What a goalie!
Parent 3:	Yeah, she's really **on her game** today.
Parent 2:	Jason's **gonna** be **ticked off** that he didn't get that goal.

Words and phrases

Match the words in the list to the correct definition:

breakaway

deke

save

ticked off

a) when a goalie stops the puck from entering the net

b) when a player has a clear way to the goal, with no defensive players blocking

c) upset or angry

d) a move where a player makes a fake shot or movement to draw a defending player out of position.

Follow-up

1. In your own words, explain the action on the ice at the hockey game.

2. Do you enjoy watching or playing hockey? Discuss what you like and what you don't like about the game.

3. Both boys and girls are playing in this hockey game. Sometimes younger children play on mixed teams, while older children play on all boys' or all girls' teams. Some girls have demanded the right to play on boys' teams. Do you think some girls can/should play on boys' teams?

4. Discuss the advantages and disadvantages of structured activities for children. Structured activities include music lessons, sports, and arts and crafts classes.

ON AND OFF AND ON AGAIN

Many expressions using **on** and **off** express the basic meaning of power being on or off. Electric appliances such as lights and radios are **turned on** and **off**. In the dialogue, a different meaning is shown when the goalie is said to be "on her game."

On is used for performances. A stage actor might be told, "You're **on** in five minutes." This meaning is extended to everyday life: if someone is **on** all the time, he or she seems to be performing for an audience. Similarly, you might ask, "What's **on**?" when you want to know what programs are playing on television.

If something continues for a long time, it goes **on and on**. Something that is not consistent might be described as **off and on** (or **on and off**, which means the same thing). A relationship might be described as **on again, off again**.

SPORTS SURVEY

Find out which sports are the most popular among your classmates, friends, and relatives.

Here are some questions you can ask:

What sport do you most enjoy playing?

What sport do you most enjoy watching?

Did you play a sport when you were a child? Which one?

Do you play a sport regularly now? Which one?

What sports do your children play?

Make a list of the sports you found to be popular now. Do you think these sports are more popular now than they were in the past? In groups, discuss what makes a sport popular.

GOOD FENCES MAKE GOOD NEIGHBOURS?

Here are some problems that neighbours might face. In small groups, discuss what you could do in each situation. Role-play conversations that you might have with the neighbour or with someone in authority.

Your neighbour plays loud music at night.

Your neighbour's yard is a mess. The grass is long and full of weeds, and garbage is spread all around.

Your neighbour's dog barks all night.

In your apartment building, children are playing loudly in the hallways and are fooling around with the elevator.

Neighbourhood pets are digging in your garden.

Your neighbours are not clearing their sidewalks in the winter.

What are some other problems neighbours could have? How can people be good neighbours?

THE DAILY NEWSPAPER

Newspapers are a valuable source of information for every community. Major **dailies** (daily newspapers) include local news, but smaller community newspapers may also be published once or twice a week, or less often. In your community paper, you can read the results of high school sports and notices from your local government. These papers are often delivered free with advertising flyers.

The "Letters to the Editor" section is usually in the front section (the main news section of the newspaper), on the editorial page. In this section the newspaper prints letters from readers, commenting on stories that have appeared in the paper.

Bring current local newspapers to class. In small groups, identify the major sections of each paper. If you have more than one local newspaper, compare them. Identify which sections of the newspaper are most useful to you. Report to the class on what you think are the most valuable features of your local newspaper.

A LETTER TO THE EDITOR

Dear Editor:

I was disappointed to read that the **municipal council** wants to **scrap** plans for extensions of the city's **bike paths**. This is an extremely **short-sighted** decision.

In Halcyon Hills, the bike path passes through most of the community. This path is extremely well used. It is convenient as well as recreational. Many people travel to the library, the mall, and the rec centre by bicycle.

It's true that bike paths are expensive to build and maintain. But people who use bicycles instead of cars are healthier. With more people cycling, pollution is also decreased and that benefits everyone. Moreover, bicycle paths are good for community spirit; they bring people together.

Municipal council should realize the benefits of bike paths and **rethink** this decision.

Jacqueline Carstairs

Words and phrases

1. The expression "to **scrap** something" is informal English. Can you think of other ways to say the same thing?

2. The prefix **re-** in front of a word means "again." (**Rethink** means "think again." It is an informal expression.) Make a list of ten words that have this prefix. Then, check the words in the dictionary.

Follow-up

1. What is the news story that Jacqueline Carstairs is reacting to?

2. Why does she think the plan is "short-sighted"? Explain her opinion.

3. Do you have bike paths in your community? What are the advantages and disadvantages of bike paths?

4. Pick a news story that interests you and write a letter to the editor giving your opinion.

THE LONG AND THE SHORT OF IT

Short-sighted means "to have short sight." It can refer to actual vision or to the idea that someone is not looking far into the future. Several words have a similar form. For example, the opposite of short-sighted is **far-sighted**.

Match the words with the definitions:

broad-minded	near-sighted
far-sighted	short-handed
long-winded	short-lived
narrow-minded	short-tempered

a) lacking staff

b) needing glasses to see things far away, only able to see up close

c) needing glasses to see things close up

d) not lasting a long time

e) not accepting other points of view

f) quick to get angry

g) talking a long time without stopping

h) willing to accept new ideas

GARAGE SALES

Use the words in the list below to fill in the blanks in the reading passage.

auctions	recycle
bargain	rummage sales
brand-new	second-hand
moving sale	surplus
outgrow	yard sales

Garage sales have become very popular in Canada. People want to _____ things they no longer need, instead of throwing more into the garbage. In addition, people can save money by buying _____ goods.

Items sold at garage sales vary. You can buy clothing, toys, books, kitchen wares, and home decorations. Because children _____ clothes and toys so quickly, you will find a lot of these items for sale. Sometimes you find _____ things: people may sell something they received as a gift and never used, or people who have their own **retail** business may sell off _____ goods at their garage sales.

Usually, items sold at garage sales are priced very cheaply. In fact, many things can be bought for less than a dollar. People often try to _____ , offering a lower price.

Since goods are usually displayed outdoors, garage sales are sometimes called _____ . A _____ occurs when people wish to sell their furniture and household items before they move; these sales may be inside the house.

Second-hand goods are also sold by charities or as a business. Sometimes churches and community groups hold _____; people in the community donate the things that are sold, and the money is used for charity. Professional dealers may organize **flea markets**. _____ are professionally organized also, but in these events the buyers must **bid** for the goods.

In the passage above, find three words that are used instead of "things."

Have you ever held a garage sale? What kind of sales have you attended? What is the best bargain you found?

LET'S HAVE A GARAGE SALE

Raj: Hi, Jake. Here's the ladder I borrowed. Thanks a lot. It really **came in handy** when I painted the stairwell.

Jake: No problem. I'm glad you had some use for it. Now if only I could find a place to put it. (*He looks around at his full and messy garage.*)

Raj: **Whoa.** What's going on here? Did a tornado hit this place?

Jake: I know, I know—it's a mess. I'm trying to **spring clean**. But once I pulled the stuff off the shelves, I couldn't decide what to do with it, so—

Raj: You don't need all this junk. Just get rid of it. Have a garage sale—clear the place out and make a few **bucks** too.

Jake: I've thought about it. I**'ve got** the kids' old stuff to get rid of. But we never **get around to** arranging it all.

Raj: We could both have garage sales.

Jake: Not a bad idea. Hmm, maybe some of the other people on the street would be interested too. A street sale attracts more customers.

Raj: OK. Let's mention it to the neighbours.

Jake: You think I could find a buyer for this old camping-stove?

Raj: Why not? You know what they say: one person's junk is another's treasure.

Words and phrases

1. How is **spring cleaning** different from regular house cleaning?

2. **Bucks** is slang for dollars or money. Do you know any other slang terms for money?

Follow-up

1. Where does the dialogue take place? Why has Raj come to see Jake?

2. What is Raj surprised about? What does he suggest?

3. Explain the expression "one person's junk is another's treasure." Give examples.

CONTRACTIONS AND "HAVE GOT"

Contractions are a common feature of everyday speech. People usually shorten auxiliary (helping) verbs such as **have**, **be**, **will**, and **would**.

Review your knowledge of these verbs by writing the long form for each contracted form in the sentences below:

1. I**'d** rather see the movie downtown.

2. He**'ll** be taking the train this time.

3. They**'ve** been to Vancouver before.

4. She**'s** taking the seven o'clock flight.

5. I**'m** sure that it **won't** take much time.

6. She**'s** a lawyer.

7. Marie**'s** going to Newfoundland for a holiday.

8. You**'re** sure you want to go tomorrow?

9. I should**'ve** taken the train instead.

10. They**'re** buying a new house.

What is the main verb in each sentence?

The verb **to have** is not contracted when it is the main verb (not an auxiliary verb).

I have five dollars in my pocket.

but not   I've five dollars in my pocket.

In informal English, people often use the contracted form of **have** with **got** to mean "have."

I've got five dollars in my pocket.

This form can be confusing, because **got** also means **receive** or **obtain**.

I've got a new book. = I have a new book.

I got a new book. = I received a new book.

BARGAINING

Offering a lower price for something is considered acceptable in some situations, but may not be acceptable in others. Bargaining practices vary from culture to culture. Canadians generally **make a deal** when they buy houses and cars. However, bargaining is rare in retail stores, unless the item is "on clearance" or damaged.

In groups, discuss bargaining in Canada and in your native country. For example, when have you purchased something for less than the advertised price? When do you bargain for a lower price? What are good situations to bargain in? What might someone say when they want to offer a lower price for something?

RECYCLING

The disposal of garbage is a major problem in Canada. Some garbage is burned and some is buried in **landfill** sites, but people do not want **incinerators** or **dumps** near their homes. Most people agree, however, that the best solution is to **cut down on** (reduce) the amount of garbage that is produced. Recycling and reusing objects and materials is encouraged.

In small groups, discuss things that can be recycled. Can you find another use for these items?

• old televisions, radios, stereos

- paper (such as your old school notes and photocopies)
- egg cartons
- fall leaves
- vegetable scraps from the kitchen
- plastic pop bottles
- clothes that are worn or that no longer fit

Do you have any other suggestions for reducing the amount of garbage we produce?

COME INTO MY NEIGHBOURHOOD

What are the good points of your neighbourhood? Is it in a good location? Are the people friendly? Are the facilities good? Are the buildings attractive?

Prepare a list of the things you like about your neighbourhood. Work with a partner to "sell" your neighbourhood. Try to convince your classmate to move next door to you. Explain what is good about the area and answer any questions your partner may have.

Afterwards, switch roles so that your partner talks about the advantages of his or her community while you ask questions.

MORE TO DO

1. Take a tour of your city hall. Arrange a tour as a class field trip or go individually.

2. Hold a school garage sale or rummage sale. You can bring in a few items from home that you no longer need. The sale can be a fund-raising event: items can be donated, and the money raised can pay for a school activity or it can go to a charity.

In the Mall

THE MALL AS COMMUNITY CENTRE

You can do more than just shop in North American shopping malls. You can watch a movie, attend a lecture, borrow a book, ride a carousel, report a crime, or even go skating. Someone can take care of your children while you shop. You can have your teeth fixed or have your will drawn up. The mall has become both a public meeting place and an entertainment centre.

The **lure** of the mall is so great that downtown stores find it hard to attract business. In suburban areas, office buildings and condominiums are **clustered** around malls. The city hall may even be located near a mall rather than downtown. It is not surprising that some malls are named "town centres."

Teenagers often use the mall as the local "**hangout**," even though mall management discourages **loitering** in public areas. Instead, some malls offer **drop-in centres** for teens. School has even been brought to the mall as an attempt to reach students who **drop out** of regular classes. After all, what better place to study **retailing** than in a place where it actually happens?

Special programs are not only offered to young people: adults may join walking clubs and get their morning exercise **striding** past stores not yet open.

Some of these activities seem to be misplaced in such an **artificial** and **commercial** environment as a mall. Yet malls offer shoppers convenience as well as protection from the weather, so they will continue to be places where people get together.

Follow-up

1. Here is a list of businesses or facilities that may be found in a mall. Match each one to the activities mentioned in the first paragraph.

   amusement park

   auditorium

   cinema

   daycare centre

   dentist's office

   lawyer's office

   library

   police station

   rink

2. What does your local mall offer?

3. What do you like or dislike about shopping malls?

PLAYING THE LOTTERY

In shopping centres people can usually buy lottery tickets at information booths. Lotteries are very popular, and people can buy different kinds of tickets. They can choose their own numbers, buy numbered tickets, or play **scratch-and-win** games.

Lotteries are **controversial**. Some people view them as a good way for the government to make money. Other people regard gambling as **immoral** and **addictive** and believe that the government should not support such an activity. Moreover, many people waste money buying lottery tickets that they cannot **afford**. They have very little chance of winning a big prize.

BUYING A DREAM

Yasmin: **Hang on** a **sec**, Micki. I want to buy my lottery ticket for Saturday's **draw**.

Micki: You buy lottery tickets?

Yasmin: Sure — **every now and then**.

Micki: It's a waste of money, you know. Your chances of winning are so small—you have a better chance of being hit by lightning.

Yasmin:	Yeah, yeah, I know. I've heard all that. But for the few dollars I spend, I **figure** it's cheap entertainment.
Micki:	Entertainment?
Yasmin:	Yeah, sometimes I sit back and **daydream** about what I'd do if I actually did win a big prize. I design my dream house, plan my trip around the world—that sort of thing.
Micki:	I guess everyone does that once in a while—as long as you don't live with your **head in the clouds**.
Yasmin:	Don't worry, I'm a **realist**. I know my chances of becoming rich are much better if I work hard than if I buy lottery tickets. But it's still fun to try.

Words and phrases

Match the words in the list to the correct definition:

addictive

afford

controversial

daydream

every now and then

hang on

having your head in the clouds

immoral

realist

sec

a) occasionally, once in a while

b) causing disagreement, argument or debate

c) always dreaming, unrealistic, not practical

d) causing a habit that is hard to break

e) not right, not good, going against principles

f) wait (informal)

g) a short period of time, a second (shortened form, informal)

h) imagine pleasant ideas of how your life could be

i) practical person, not a dreamer

j) have enough money to buy something

Follow-up

1. Why does Yasmin buy lottery tickets?

2. Why does Micki think buying lottery tickets is a bad idea?

3. Which expression describes you more accurately: do you have your head in the clouds or your feet on the ground?

4. Do you buy lottery tickets? Why or why not?

5. Look at some advertisements (in newspapers and magazines and on television) for lotteries. How do they try to encourage people to buy tickets?

6. Money is a popular subject for songs. Try to find recordings of some of the songs in the list below (or other songs on similar themes) and listen to them in class. Discuss the main idea of the songs.

    "If I had $1,000,000" — Barenaked Ladies

    "If I were a rich man" — from the musical *Fiddler on the Roof*

    "Can't buy me love" — the Beatles

    "The Money Song" — from the musical *Cabaret*

WHAT WOULD YOU DO?

In "Buying a Dream," Yasmin says, "I sit back and daydream about what **I'd** do if I actually did win a big prize." "I'd" is a contraction of "I would."

Would is an auxiliary verb used in conditional sentences in English. The imaginative conditional means that what a person wishes for is not possible or not likely to happen right away. Here are some examples of this imaginative conditional:

> If I had a million dollars, I would buy a sailboat and sail around the world.

> If I had a pilot's licence, I would commute to work by plane.

> If I had a computer, I'd be able to do these essays faster.

> If I was rich, I'd have a huge house with a swimming pool.*

> If I were rich, I'd have a huge house with a swimming pool.*

The **if** clause has a verb in the past tense, even though the idea of the sentence is not a past action.

Practise the conditional form by telling what you would do if you won the lottery.

GAMBLING IDIOMS

Many English idioms come from gambling and games. For example, you **bet** on something when you are so sure of the result that you will risk money on it. "I bet" is a very common expression which means "I'm sure." "You bet" and "you betcha" both mean "of course" or "certainly."

> I **bet** I can run faster than you.

> He **bet** that the Blue Jays would win the World Series again.

Card games, such as poker and blackjack, are commonly used for gambling. If you have an **ace up your sleeve**, you have a secret plan or something in reserve. If all your **cards are on the table**, you are not hiding anything.

Bingo is a popular activity in many communities. It may be played in church basements, community centres, malls, or special bingo halls. The cry "**Bingo!**" announces a win in the game, but it is also used in other situations to mean "I've done it" or "I've got it."

*The structure "If I were" is a subjunctive. The subjunctive is a form that is dying in English. Many people say "If I was" in this conditional sentence, even though some people think this is ungrammatical.

hanging around with

Similarly, a **jackpot** is the prize in many games. If you say that you **hit the jackpot** it means that you have had great success at something.

Follow-up

1. Discuss games and gambling. Is gambling acceptable in your native country? Some religions have strict rules regarding games and gambling; do you know any of these rules? What forms of betting are popular in your native country?

2. Gambling can be an addiction. What are the dangers of being addicted to gambling?

HANGING AROUND WITH "HANG"

The verb **hang** is generally used to refer to objects that are fastened at the top and can swing freely. For instance, you **hang up** your clothes and you **hang** pictures on a wall.

Hang shows variations of this basic meaning in phrasal verbs and other expressions:

The mall is a **hang-out** for young people. In other words, it is a place where they like to get together and spend time.

When Yasmin wants to buy lottery tickets, she tells Micki to wait, saying "**hang on.**"

You can **hang around** a place or **hang around with** a person. In both cases, the action is habitual: you are in the place often or you are with the person often.

In giving directions, you might tell someone to **hang a right** or **hang a left** when it is time for them to turn.

You **hang up** the phone when you finish talking.

You **get the hang of something** when you learn how to do it.

Fill in the blanks in the following sentences with phrasal verbs and expressions with **hang**.

1. I tried to explain the problem on the phone, but he just _hung up_ . He still won't talk to me.

2. She's trying to teach me the butterfly stroke in swimming class, but I just can't _get the hang of it_

3. You can _hang up_ your jacket on that rack.

4. She told me to _hang on_ while she looked for the right report.

5. I'm worried about my son. I don't like the kids he's been _hanging around with_ lately.

6. At the first set of lights, _hang a right_ at Browning Street.

7. Oops, I've got another call coming in. Can you just _hang on_ a second while I check if it's the call I've been waiting for?

BANKING TERMS

Use the words below to fill in the blanks in the paragraphs describing banking services.

    access code
    account
    branch
    deposit
    loans
    tellers
    transfer funds
    withdrawal

If you want to use banking services, first you have to open an _____ . Generally, you do your banking at one _____ of the bank, usually a location near your home or your work.

When you make your transactions in the bank, you deal with the _____. These people give you money when you make a _____ from your account or take your money when you make a _____. If you have chequing and savings accounts, you might have to _____ between accounts.

Some people prefer to do their banking electronically or by telephone. When you sign up to use the bank machine service, you are given a card and an _____, which is your secret identification number.

Bank machines have different names. Your bank might call it an ATM (Automatic Teller Machine) or an ABM (Automatic Bank Machine). In everyday speech, people use the general term "bank machine" or they use the brand name of their bank's ATM. For example, they might say, "I need to go to the Instabank" or "I'm looking for the Green Machine."

In addition to the everyday transactions, you may deal with other bank officers to arrange _loan_, make investments, rent a safety deposit box, and use other banking services.

USING A BANK MACHINE

David: Oh no. Look at that **line-up** in the bank. I want to deposit a cheque, but I don't want to wait that long.

Rico: Why don't you just use the machine to make your deposit?

David: I don't like bank machines. I prefer dealing with human beings.

Rico: But it's so convenient. You don't have to worry about whether the bank is open or not. And it's great when you travel.

David: Oh, I'd probably **screw it all up**. I'd punch in the wrong numbers or something.

Rico: It's not hard. Step-by-step instructions guide you through the process, and if you make a mistake you can press the cancel button to stop the transaction.

David: Maybe I will **give it a shot**. Anything to avoid these line-ups.

Words and phrases

1. In this dialogue, **line-up** is used as a noun. Form a sentence using the verb form, "to line up." Do you know another word that means **line-up**? (hint: it starts with "q")

2. **To screw something up** and **to give something a shot** are two slang expressions. Choose the right meaning for each expression from the list below:

to do a good job

to try to do something

to ask a question

to make a mistake

to understand something

Follow-up

1. Why is David reluctant to use a bank machine? What does he worry about?

2. What arguments does Rico use to convince David?

3. Do you prefer going to a teller or using a bank machine? Why?

4. Do you know people who are afraid of using modern technology, such as computers, answering machines, and bank machines? Discuss.

FAST FOOD, JUNK FOOD, GOOD FOOD?

Shopping malls have many different kinds of food services, including full-service restaurants and cafeterias in department stores. A selection of fast-food **outlets** may be grouped together in a **food court**. Most food courts have a large central seating area, and shoppers can choose their meals from different businesses. Varieties of **fast food** available include pizza, hamburgers, frozen yogurt, exotic fruit juices, coffee and doughnuts, and Chinese food.

Fast food includes restaurant food such as hamburgers and pizza. **Junk food** is food with little **nutritional** value, such as potato chips, candy, and pop. Some people consider fast foods to be junk foods, but pizza and hamburgers do contain **protein** and **vitamins**, even though they are high in fat.

Many Canadians worry about nutrition. They try to avoid foods that are high in fat or sugar. They also try to eat more foods that are high in **fibre**, such as cereals and whole-wheat bread.

Visit a mall food court or your school cafeteria and make a list of food that is good for your health and food that you would consider **junk food**.

EATING AT THE FOOD COURT

Thomas: OK, so what do you want to eat? Pizza? Mexican food? Hamburgers?

Eliza: I don't know, I can't decide between a Japanese **stir-fry** or **fish 'n chips**.

Thomas: Fish 'n chips? You're kidding. You usually stay away from **deep-fried** foods.

Eliza: I know, but once in a while I get a **craving**. And they have really good English-style fish 'n chips here.

Thomas: So go ahead. We deserve a treat. With all the walking we've been doing, we'll burn off the calories **in no time**.

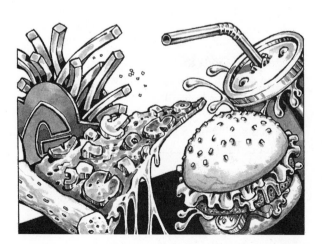

Words and phrases

1. How is **stir-frying** different from **deep-frying**?

2. How are **fish 'n chips** prepared?

Follow-up

1. What is Eliza's dilemma?

2. What kind of food do you order in a food court? Do you like eating there?

3. Do you ever have a craving for certain kinds of food? For example, do you ever crave chocolate or something salty?

4. What food is a special treat for you?

5. Visit a local mall and make a list of the kinds of food outlets found there.

GOING TO THE DENTIST

Eliza: What's the matter? Isn't your meal good?

Thomas: Oh, the food's fine. It's just that my tooth is **bothering** me and it's **kinda** hard to chew.

Eliza: You've been complaining about that tooth **for ages**. Why don't you go to the dentist and get it fixed?

Thomas: I've been **meaning to**, but I haven't **gotten around to it.** I haven't had a chance to find a new dentist.

Eliza: You know, there's a dentist's office right here in the mall.

Thomas: Owwww. OK, OK, let's go **check it out**.

Later that day:

Receptionist: Yes, may I help you?

Thomas: I was wondering if I could get an appointment.

Receptionist: Are you a regular patient here?

Thomas: No, it's my first time. Aren't you taking on new patients?

Receptionist: Yes, we are. I just wanted to know if you have a **file** here. Do you want to come for a check-up or is there a specific problem?

Thomas: I have a tooth that's been **bothering** me for a while.

Receptionist: Well, if you're **free** this afternoon, we've had a **cancellation** for three o'-clock.

Thomas: That would be fine.

Words and phrases

1. What is the expression in the dialogue that means "for a very long time"? Can you think of other expressions that mean the same thing?

2. Tell the class about something you've been **meaning to do**. Why have you been **putting it off** (delaying it)? When do you think you will **get around to** doing it?

3. Here are some words associated with paper files:

   filing

   file folder

   filing cabinet

   Today, files are more likely to be kept in a computer. The icon used for files looks like a file folder:

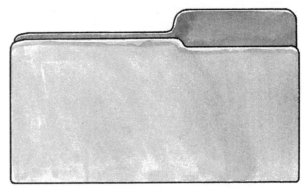

Follow-up

1. Why is Thomas not enjoying his meal?

2. What has he been putting off?

3. Why is Thomas lucky when he goes to make an appointment?

4. Do you put off going to the dentist or do you visit one regularly?

Hollywood

5. Have you ever cancelled a dentist's appointment? How much notice does your dentist ask for?

WORDS FOR THE DENTIST'S OFFICE

Fill in the blanks in the sentences with words from the list below. Other useful words are marked in bold.

     baby teeth

     braces

     cavities

     crown

     dental hygienist

     freezing

     molar

     toothache

     wisdom teeth

1. When we are about six years old, we start losing our _____.

2. The _____ cleans your teeth and gives them a **fluoride treatment** to help prevent **decay**.

3. When I was a teenager, I had to wear ugly metal _____, but I guess it was worth it now. I have fewer problems with my teeth now that they're straight.

4. My tooth has to be **capped** with a _____. I decided to get a gold one since it's in the back and won't show too much.

5. I hate getting **fillings**. The **drill** doesn't bother me, but I don't like getting needles for _____ my mouth.

6. The back teeth are called _____.

7. I just had a dental **check-up**—no ____!

8. I have such a terrible ____. I need to **make an appointment** with my dentist right away.

9. Young adults often get new molars, but these ____ sometimes get **pulled**.

ANSWERING QUESTIONS IN THE NEGATIVE

Yes–no questions that contain a negative can be very confusing. Questions are phrased in the negative because the speaker expects a positive, or **yes**, answer.

Some languages have special response words to contradict a negative question. In English, however, whether you use **yes** or **no** depends on the answer, not on the form of the question.

Don't you have any change?	Yes, (I do have change).
	No, (I don't have change).

To avoid confusion, people often answer a negative question with a phrase rather than with just the single word **yes** or **no**. In the dialogue "Going to the Dentist," how does the receptionist answer Thomas's negative question?

Practise asking and answering negative questions with a partner. You can talk about your food likes and dislikes or your shopping practices.

MARKETING IN GROCERY STORES

Use the words in the list to fill in the blanks in the following passage:

     aisles

     appeal

     aroma

     checkout

     impulse

     likely

     packaged

     pricing

When you go to a grocery store, you enter a world that has been carefully arranged to encourage you to make _____ purchases and spend more money than you planned.

As you approach the store, you may smell the enticing _____ of fresh baked bread. Near the entrances you will usually see displays of fresh fruit and vegetables or a deli and meat counter, because fresh food is more attractive than _____, prepared foods.

As you push your cart up and down the _____, you notice the more expensive brands of foods at your eye-level. Cheaper brands are usually at the bottom of the shelf.

The _____ of items is also significant. $2.99 seems a lot cheaper than $3.00, because you associate it with $2 rather than $3. When items are priced at 3 for 99 cents, you are _____ to buy three even if you only need one.

The names of products and the design of packaging are carefully chosen to _____ to consumers. Cleaning products, for example, have short, strong names. Laundry detergent is found in green, blue, or yellow boxes. Foods have **homey**, personal names (like "Mrs. Brown's Soup") to make you think of home-cooking.

Near the _____, you see racks full of magazines and candy; both are small, inexpensive items that people are likely to buy on impulse.

Check it out

1. Arrange a class tour of a nearby grocery store or visit one on your own. Look for the marketing techniques mentioned above. In small groups, discuss what you learned on your visit. What do you like about the grocery store, and what do you not like? Compare this grocery store with others you have visited.

2. Choose a grocery-store product, such as breakfast cereal or frozen pizza. Visit a grocery store to look at a number of different brands. Write down the names of the products, the types of packages, and the colours used on the box. Are there any common trends that you notice? Report your findings to the class.

GENERIC AND BRAND NAMES

A **brand name** is a name that a company has chosen for its product or products. It is a **registered trademark**, which belongs to the company. The use of the name is controlled; the company must give permission for its use.

Generic name is the opposite of brand name. **Generic** refers to the product in general. For example, many grocery stores stock products that are labelled only with generic names, such as "green beans" or "potato chips," without a specific company's name.

Sometimes the brand name becomes the common name for that type of article. For example, most people say "Kleenex" rather than "tissue," even though "Kleenex" is a specific brand of tissue. These brand names can even become verbs; people may say they are "Xeroxing" something, instead of "photocopying" it.

Because of the laws controlling trademarks, brand names cannot be freely used in publications or broadcasts. However, in everyday speech, the brand names have become part of the language.

Can you give a generic name for the brand names in the following list?

Aspirin

Coke

Jello

Rollerblades

Saran Wrap

Scotch tape

Skidoo

Styrofoam

Thermos

THE ART OF COMPLAINING

Complaint letters are an important part of doing business. Managers appreciate customer **feedback** on their services and products—whether the letters are complaints or compliments. This feedback is important because it tells managers what needs to be changed and what works well. Business people also like to have the opportunity to make dissatisfied customers happy.

A LETTER OF COMPLAINT

111 Main Street,
Halifax, N.S.
January 2, 1997

Manager
Cinema World
Rockwood Mall
Halifax, N.S.

Dear Sir or Madam:

Yesterday my husband and I attended a showing of *Max and Moxie* at the Cinema World theatre at Rockwood Mall. It was not a pleasant experience.

The quality of the film itself was poor. The scratches and spots totally **distracted** me. I barely saw the movie. Moreover, the sound quality was poor.

This was my first visit to Cinema World as we have just moved to this area. However, I do not think I will return.

Sincerely,

Sophia Peters

Follow-up

1. Why does Ms. Peters write to the Cinema World theatre? Do you think she has the right to complain? What do you think the manager should do?

2. Have you ever had an experience like this in a movie theatre? What other kinds of problems have you had while watching a movie?

3. In small groups, discuss services and products at your local mall. Do you have any complaints or compliments that you think should be passed on to the management?

4. The manager of Cinema World sent a letter of apology to Ms. Peters, explaining that the theatre replaced the poor print of the movie with a better one. The manager also sent her two free passes to the theatre. Ms. Peters went to another movie, enjoyed it, and wrote a thank-you letter to the manager. Write the manager's letter of apology and Ms. Peters's thank-you letter.

MORE TO DO

1. In small groups, talk about your city's or region's shopping areas. How many major malls are there? Are they well located? Have malls affected the downtown shopping area? Is there a farmer's market? What are the most popular shopping areas?

2. As a class project, write a booklet or make an informative video containing shopping hints. Include information on the best places to shop, how to use coupons, how to look for sales, and other ways to be a good bargain-hunter.

At Work

THE CANADIAN WORKPLACE

The Canadian **workplace** is constantly changing. Advances in technology mean more than just new tools for workers. Computers and robots may replace employees or dramatically change the work people do. For example, computers in offices have reduced the number of secretaries and clerks. Managers now write their own letters and memos on computers.

Poor economic conditions have forced many businesses to **lay off** employees. Employers find it less expensive to keep a smaller staff and hire part-time and contract workers when necessary. As a result, many people have to make their own jobs. They work as **consultants** or **freelancers**, or start their own small businesses.

Education is the key to helping the workforce deal with changing situations. Some people go back to school to learn new skills. Some change their careers completely. **In-house** training sessions and **workshops** may train employees to use new software. **Conferences** are another way that professionals learn about developments in their field. Workers are anxious to keep up with the changing workplace.

Follow-up

1. What is the main point of "The Canadian Workplace"? What is the main point of each paragraph?

2. Why is new technology important in the workplace?

3. Why are more people starting their own businesses?

4. How do workers keep up with the changes in the workplace?

5. What kind of changes have you seen in the workplace? Discuss the effects of these changes.

STARTING A SMALL BUSINESS

Hans: Robin, you know how we've talked about me starting up a **landscaping** business? Well, it looks like it's **gonna** be sooner rather than later.

Robin: Why? What happened?

Hans: The **nursery**'s going **belly-up**. We'll all be getting **pink slips** soon.

Robin: Oh, no. How are we going to manage without your job?

Hans: It'll be **tough** for a while, but we can survive on your income, I think. And, hey, this might be just the opportunity we've been waiting for.

Robin: I don't know, Hans. Starting a business—it's so expensive.

Hans: The nursery'll be **liquidating its stock** and I can probably pick up some tools and such. And I don't need much of an office since I'll go out to my clients.

Robin: But there are other **start-up costs**— business cards, advertising...

Hans: Hey, that's where **it comes in handy** to have a brother-in-law in the printing business.

Words and phrases

Match the words and phrases with the correct definition.

comes in handy   nursery

go belly-up   pink slip

landscaping   start-up costs

liquidated   tough

a) place where plants and trees are grown and sold; also a place for children

b) arranging trees, shrubs, and flowers in an area to make a pleasing appearance

c) becomes useful (informal)

d) the notice employees receive when they are fired or laid-off from a job

e) difficult, hard (informal)

f) sold to get quick cash

g) expenses of beginning a business

h) go out of business, die (slang)

Follow-up

1. What kind of business does Hans want to start? What do you know about this type of work?

2. What advantages does Hans have in starting his business?

3. What is Robin worried about?

4. Why is Hans pleased that his brother-in-law is in the printing business?

5. What kind of problems might Hans have in starting his business? What else does he need to think about?

6. Discuss the advantages and disadvantages of running a small business. Have you or your family ever had your own business? Tell about your experience.

SICK LEAVE

Sick-leave benefits are determined by the contract an employee has. **Salaried workers** are allowed a certain number of sick days a year, and their pay is not affected. However, other employees are only paid for the hours they work; they lose money when they are off sick.

CALLING IN SICK

Rebecca: Information services. Rebecca Mayhew speaking.

Paul: Hello, Rebecca, this is Paul. **I'm afraid** I won't be coming in to work today.

Rebecca: Paul, you sound terrible! What's wrong?

Paul: I think I **caught** that **bug** that's been going around.

Rebecca: That's too bad. It's awful—**fever, nausea, the whole bit**. I guess you won't be in for a couple of days.

Paul: I hope it won't take that long. I've got that report to prepare for next week.

Rebecca: Well, come in when you're feeling better. At least you don't have to worry about giving it to anyone else: I think everyone has had it now.

Paul: Gee, thanks. You sure know how to make someone feel better.

Rebecca: Cheer up. Maybe we'll even send you some flowers.

Words and phrases

1. In English, you **catch** a cold. What else can you catch?

2. **Bug** is a slang term that has several meanings. What does it mean in the dialogue?

3. What are the signs of a **fever**? Which of the following expressions mean that the person might have a fever:

   I've got a temperature.

   He's shivering so much his teeth are chattering.

   She looks flushed.

   Her forehead's hot.

   He gets hot under the collar easily.

Follow-up

1. Why is Paul calling his office?

2. Is Rebecca **sympathetic** (does she feel sorry for him)?

3. What does Rebecca know about the illness Paul has?

4. Some people hate to miss work and go in even when they are very sick. On the other hand, some people believe that a little rest at the beginning of an illness may prevent it from getting worse. Some people stay home only if they have a **contagious** illness (one that can be easily passed to other people). What guidelines would you give for someone deciding whether or not to call in sick?

5. What remedies and treatments do you use for colds and flu? Do you have any family or herbal cures?

POLITE EXPRESSIONS

When Paul calls in sick, he says, "**I'm afraid** I won't be coming in to work today." "I'm afraid" is a polite, softening expression which is used to introduce some bad news, something the other person would not like to hear.

Here are other examples:

I'm sorry to say I can't attend the meeting.

I regret to say that we cannot give you a raise this year.

TALKING ABOUT YOUR ACHES AND PAINS

Despite its name, a **cold** does not come from being cold. You might get a **chill** from the cold weather, but colds and flu are caused by **germs** that are spread by other people. Illnesses have different **symptoms** (visible signs).

A cold or the **flu** (short for **influenza**) may be called a **bug**. If you have a cold, you might **cough** or **sneeze**. Coughing and sneezing spread germs. You may also have a **sore throat**.

Nausea is the feeling of sickness where you could **vomit**. Colloquial terms for vomiting include **throwing up** and **being sick to your stomach**.

Headaches are common, everyday illnesses. Other types of common aches and pains are **stomachaches, backaches, toothaches,** and **earaches**.

Fill in the blanks in the example sentences below using the words in the list.

backache

chills

cough

germs

laryngitis

sneeze

symptoms

toothache

1. I have to make an appointment with the dentist. I have a _____ .

2. After the car accident, I had a constant _____ . It made it difficult to sit for long periods of time.

3. You should wash your hands often so you don't spread _____ .

4. The professor had to cancel class because he had _____ and couldn't talk.

5. His cold affected his lungs and he had a loud _____ for weeks afterwards.

6. I'm allergic to cats. Cat hair makes me _____ .

7. When you go to the doctor, he asks about your _____ . Then he tells you what is wrong with you.

8. She had the _____ so bad that she was shivering and her teeth were chattering.

Identify different situations in which you might talk about an illness, and discuss what is appropriate or polite in these situations. For example, a friend might not want to hear every detail about your illness, but your doctor needs specific information.

NO SMOKING ALLOWED

Smoking areas are controlled by **by-laws** (laws made by local governments). In many Canadian cities, smoking is not allowed in public buildings or is restricted to certain areas. Many workplaces have been designated "smoke-free."

Anti-smoking laws are **controversial.** Smokers insist that they should have the right to smoke in public areas. However, it is generally agreed that **smoke-free** environments are healthier for everyone.

Follow-up

1. Do you think smoking should be allowed in public areas?

2. What are the by-laws in your area? For example, is smoking allowed in hospitals?

NO SMOKING IN THE WORKPLACE

Mustafa: Did you hear **the latest**? They're going to make this whole building smoke-free next year.

Dennis: You're kidding. No place to smoke? Not even this little corner of the cafeteria?

Mustafa: That's right.

Dennis: **There's no way** I'm **gonna** go outside every time I want **a smoke.**

Mustafa: What choice do we have? Look for another job?

Dennis: **No good.** All the companies are doing the same thing.

Mustafa: Maybe I could try quitting again.

Dennis: Yeah, might be an idea. I heard cigarette taxes are going up again next year.

Words and phrases

1. **Latest** is an adjective, but in this context a noun is implied in the meaning. This is an example of an **ellipsis**; in other words, something has been cut out of the original expression. What noun is understood to follow **the latest** in the dialogue?

2. **A smoke** is an idiom. What is another way to say the same thing?

3. When Dennis suggests looking for another job, Mustafa answers "**No good.**" What other expressions could he have used?

Follow-up

1. Is Dennis surprised to hear about the loss of a smoking area within the building?

2. Cutting down on smoking areas is usually a gradual process. What steps did this company take?

3. What do you think is the best way to quit smoking? Some people reduce their cigarette intake gradually, while others quit **cold turkey**. ("Cold turkey" is an idiom which means that you give up a habit completely and suddenly.)

THE SMOKING CONTROVERSY

Here are some statements about smoking issues. Do you agree or disagree with the statements? Support your opinion.

Cigarette advertising does not encourage people to start smoking; it only promotes different brands of cigarettes.

Each building should have a smoking area.

Warning signs on cigarettes are not effective.

Tobacco companies should not sponsor sporting events.

High taxes should be placed on cigarettes.

ADVERBS AT WORK

Adverbs are descriptive words. They describe the way an action is done. Many adverbs are formed by adding -ly to the end of an adjective.

Here are some adverbs that describe how work can be done. Match the adverb with its meaning; from the list, pick the best definition you can find. (If you do not know the adverb, look for clues. You may recognize a root word in the adverb.)

The employees did their work:

accurately	industriously
efficiently	methodically
enthusiastically	promptly
indifferently	sloppily

a) carefully and exactly with good attention to detail; making no mistakes

b) eagerly; with strong interest

c) making careless mistakes

d) not caring about the result

e) right away; without waiting

f) using an ordered system

g) well; without wasting time or effort

h) working hard, with a lot of effort

Write a paragraph describing someone's work habits. Use some of the adjectives above, as well as other expressions you know.

JOB HUNTING

Work in groups to put together advice for people looking for a job. Each group can deal with different steps in the job-hunting process. After the discussion, each group can summarize the advice and report to the class.

Here are some different aspects of job hunting that you can talk about:

- finding places to apply for a job
- filling out an application form
- writing job application letters
- writing a résumé
- preparing for an interview
- being interviewed
- adding to your job skills, getting more training and experience
- looking for a new job when you already have a job

A RÉSUMÉ

When you apply for a job, you may send in a letter with a résumé. A résumé is a short (1–2 page) **point-form** summary of your qualifications and skills. See the example on page 46.

Follow-up

1. What are Andrea Ventura's qualifications?

2. What kind of job do you think she is looking for?

3. Discuss the layout (the organization) of this résumé. How is the information organized? What other layout could Andrea have used?

4. What information should be included in résumés? What should be left out?

Do it yourself

1. Find out more about writing résumés and cover letters for job applications. Your school career centre or guidance office may have a brochure giving information on job hunting. The Canada Employment Office is another good source of information. The library also has books on job hunting and preparing résumés.

2. Write your own résumé.

Andrea Ventura
3405 Wayside Avenue
Mississauga, Ontario
L6R 1V9
(905) 555-1090

EDUCATION

Since 1994

Seneca College, Toronto
currently in second year
Tourism & Hospitality program

1993

Meadowvale Secondary School
Mississauga, Ontario
Grade 12 diploma

WORK EXPERIENCE

Information officer
Summer, 1995

Toronto Tourism Office
Gave tourist information from downtown
booth.

Tour Guide
1993–1994

Royal Provincial Museum
Gave talks on museum artifacts.
Specialized in children's programs.

Lifeguard &
Swim Instructor
1991–1993

Meadowvale Community Pool
Worked part-time after school
and full-time in summers.

LANGUAGES

French (good) and Japanese (fair)

COMPUTER SKILLS

Word processing, basic computer
operations.

AWARDS AND CERTIFICATES

1993

Award for Academic Excellence
Meadowvale Secondary School

1991

National Life Saving certificate

THE NEW EMPLOYEE

Aaron: I just met the newest member of our staff.

Laura: Oh, yeah? And what do you think of Elizabeth?

Aaron: I think she'll **fit in** great. She's got a crazy **sense of humour**.

Laura: Oh, no. Just what I need—two of you making the same jokes.

Aaron: But I **really** like her computer.

Laura: **Figures**. Any new **gadget** in this place...

Aaron: This is **really** neat, though. Her computer has a **voice recognition system**.

Laura: Oh, yeah, that's right. Elizabeth is **legally blind** so her machine responds to voice commands and it reads text aloud to her.

Aaron: Well, she's taught it a few cute tricks. When she says a swear-word, the computer plays **soothing** music.

Words and phrases

1. What expression is **Figures** shortened from? What does it mean?

2. Give examples of **gadgets.**

Follow-up

1. What does Aaron have in common with Elizabeth?

2. Why did Aaron find her computer so interesting?

3. Why do you think Elizabeth has set up her computer to respond to swear words?

4. How can computers help people who have disabilities?

COMPUTER TALK

Fill in the blanks with the words in the list:

computer literate	keyboarding
databases	hardware
desktop publishing	programs
fonts	graphics
	spreadsheet

Computers have changed both the workplace and the English language. New words about computers enter the vocabulary faster than dictionaries can keep up with them. Some of this vocabulary is highly technical, but much of it becomes part of the everyday language. Computers are so important that everyone talks about the need to be _____ , or knowledgeable about computers.

The pieces of equipment that make up a computer are called _____ . A computer also needs **software—electronic** instructions called _____ .

What used to be called **typing** is now called _____ and **word processing**. _____ includes arranging the words on the page in an attractive **layout** and using computer-generated pictures (_____) and different print styles (_____).

Word processing is one of the most popular uses of a computer. In addition, financial statements can be prepared on a computer using a _____ , which has columns and rows of numbers. _____ are programs that store information such as client files. You can find specific files and sort them in different ways.

Follow-up

1. What kind of experience have you had with computers? Do you own a computer?

2. Name the different pieces of computer equipment. Use the pictures below or real machines in your school. Work in groups to make a vocabulary list.

See it and show it

1. Go and see a demonstration of software for the different computer functions explained above (word processing, desktop publishing, spreadsheets, and databases). Your school's computer department may be able to arrange a demonstration for your class. Friends and relatives who own computers can show you their software. Computer stores also give demonstrations of new software packages.

2. Students who are knowledgeable about computers can share their knowledge by giving short, simple talks on different computer topics, such as:

- how a computer works
- how to buy a computer
- how students can use computers
- computers and children

MODERN COMMUNICATION

Modern technology has added new ways for business people to communicate with clients and staff. Today's telephones are complicated pieces of equipment with a range of different functions. For example, people can use **teleconferencing** to talk with several callers at the same time. They can **put someone on hold** or **transfer** a call.

Voice mail is a computerized answering system that uses recorded messages. The messages tell callers to press different buttons on the phone to hear the information they require, to leave a message, or to talk to someone. **Touch-tone** phones are required to use these services, and **rotary dials** are becoming obsolete.

Written communication can also be sent by various means. A **fax** sends a picture of a document over the telephone line. Inter-office **memos** are often sent by **e-mail**: electronic mail sent on a computer network. Many companies now have access to the Internet, which means they can send e-mail outside the company, to anyone with Internet access.

The **World Wide Web** offers businesses new ways to communicate with clients and customers. Many companies operate a **web site** on the **Internet**. Their web pages can give information about their products and services. Web pages are **interactive**; customers can communicate with the company by sending e-mail requests for information or products.

Follow-up

In small groups, discuss your experience with the forms of communication mentioned. What are the advantages and disadvantages of each method?

Words and phrases

1. The word **draft** has many different meanings. Sometimes, the word is spelled **draught** in Canadian and British English. From the list of meanings of **draft**, pick the one which applies to the use in the dialogue:

    an air current

    an early version of a piece of writing

    the depth of water needed by a ship so it will not touch bottom

    liquid (usually beer) drawn from a barrel

a written order for money to be paid by the bank

2. What kinds of changes are made to a document when it is **edited**?

3. What is **jargon**? What is wrong with using jargon?

Follow-up

1. Is Alanna Romanov Harold's supervisor or his co-worker? What makes you think so?

2. What does Alanna Romanov like about the report? What does she not like?

3. What does Harold have to do now?

Try it out

1. Find out about the telephone system in your school. Look at the phones.

    Do you have to dial an extra number to reach an **outside line** (to phone outside the school)?

    Can you take more than one call on a phone at the same time?

    Can you put a call **on hold**?

    Is there a voice mail system?

    Interview people to find out how much they like the system. Make a report on the phone system.

COMMENTS BY E-MAIL

Thank you for sending me the **draft** of your report. On the whole, you've done a good job. You've covered most of the issues, and your arguments are clear and persuasive.

However, I think the report could do with some **editing**. It still contains too much **jargon**. Some people may have trouble understanding it. I've marked the text with some suggestions and comments.

If you have any questions, please give me a call. Send me your next draft as soon as you have it ready.

Alanna Romanov

2. Write a memo for one of the following situations:

- you want to schedule a meeting with your co-workers
- you ask someone to look at the new catalogue before it goes to the printers
- your staff will have to work around office renovations for a few weeks
- you recommend someone for a new position

NAME THAT JOB

In small groups, discuss the occupations of people you usually meet, see, or hear every day. For example, if you listen to the radio first thing in the morning, the radio announcer or **D.J.** (disk jockey) is the first person you hear. You might also see the bus driver or the parking-lot attendant on your way to work or school.

Work together to list the names of the occupations. For example, the person who sweeps the floors in the school is called a **janitor** or **caretaker** or **maintenance worker**.

Try to name as many occupations as you can. Include people who work in the school building whom you might not see every day. Compare your list with the other groups' lists and see which group has listed the most occupations.

A PROMOTION!

Kathy: Mom! Dad! Guess what! I got a promotion. You're looking at the new assistant manager.

Teresa: Congratulations, dear. Don't tell me you were surprised?

Kathy: Well, I wasn't really expecting it. I mean, when Chris got **called into the office** last week, he ended up getting **fired**.

James: Yes, but you got such a good **performance** evaluation last month.

Kathy: True. But that doesn't always mean anything. Sometimes I think Harrison **staffs** positions by **whim**.

Teresa: I'm sure you got this promotion on **merit**. And I think you'll do a great job.

Kathy: I sure hope so. This is just the chance I was hoping for.

Words and phrases

1. There are many words and expressions that mean that someone has lost a job. Getting **laid-off** usually means losing a job because of the company's economic conditions, but getting **fired** usually means that a person lost a job because he or she is not doing well in the company.

    Here are some example sentences that talk about someone losing a job. Discuss the examples. Which expressions are slang?

    He **got canned** because he had a bad attitude.

    When they found out about the thefts, they **dismissed** several employees.

    One-third of that department will be getting **pink slips**.

    If she comes in late once more, she'll **get sacked**.

    He was **let go** when the company was **downsized**.

2. Look up **whim, whimsy,** and **whimsical** in the dictionary.

Follow-up

1. Is Kathy surprised about her promotion?
2. How do Kathy's parents feel about her promotion?
3. How should promotions be decided? What qualities should an employer look for?
4. Have you ever changed jobs within a company? Tell about your experience.

PROVERBS

Here are some proverbs about working. In groups, discuss the meaning of each proverb. Do you agree with the idea expressed?

All work and no play makes Jack a dull boy.

Many hands make light work.

Too many cooks spoil the broth.

A bad worker always blames the tools.

Rome was not built in a day.

MORE TO DO

1. Choose an occupation you are interested in. Research the qualifications for that type of work and where people can get training. (The public library has many books on different careers.) Find out more about the job itself. If possible, interview people who have that job or visit them at work. Report your findings to the class in an oral presentation.
2. Put together a career centre for your class or school. Collect brochures and newspaper clippings with advice on looking for a job. Collect some sample job application forms. Write some tips for job hunters.

At Home

THE CANADIAN FAMILY

The home is the setting for family life, and the family is the basic unit of our society. Changes in family structure and family life affect the workplace and all other areas of society.

In a traditional family, the father goes out to work, while the mother stays at home to take care of the children and do the housework. Yet few Canadian families fit this pattern today. For example, some **households** are single-parent families. Some adults live together without getting married. Most women, including those with young children, have jobs outside the home.

The lack of stay-at-home mothers has changed many business practices. Employers may give workers **parental leave** when a baby is born. Parents may be **reluctant to** travel or work overtime. Businesses have to arrange deliveries and repairs for evenings and weekends, since there is often no one home during the day.

Most people rate their family as the most important part of their lives. Children who are well-cared-for are more likely to grow up to be good adults. Moreover, social problems such as crime and drug abuse are often linked to the absence of a **stable** home life. Family life is important to the well-being of every person in society.

Follow-up

1. How can people balance the demands of a job and a family?
2. How important is family life? Give examples and discuss.
3. What do you believe is a good family environment?
4. What useful skills did you learn in your family?

COCOONING

A caterpillar spins a cocoon and stays inside until it comes out as a butterfly or moth. Thus, the word **cocoon** is used to describe a warm, safe, **snug** home.

Today, the word **cocooning** describes how families stay at home instead of going out for meals and entertainment. For example, people rent videos to watch at home instead of going out to the movies. Businesses offer products to support this lifestyle. Restaurants and food stores offer a wide range of **take-out food** and **convenience food**. Big-screen TVs, CD players, and computers entertain people in their own homes.

Time and money are two important factors in the popularity of in-home entertainment. For example, people who spend long hours at work usually want to stay home in the evening. If they commute to work, they don't want to spend time travelling for leisure activities. Two-income families often lack the time to cook, but they have the money to pay for take-out foods. Moreover, in-home entertainment costs less than going out. Parents do not have to find and pay a babysitter. Renting videos is cheaper than going to the cinema.

Follow-up

1. Do you like "cocooning"? What would you plan for a cocooning evening?
2. Do you often eat convenience foods, like frozen dinners? Why or why not?
3. Do you like to go out or do you prefer staying at home in the evening? Why?

A WEEKEND AT HOME

Beatrix: Suzy, hi. Haven't seen you for a while.

Suzy: Yeah, I've been working a lot of over-time at work. It's been a real **mad-house** getting ready for the expansion. But everything's done now, so this weekend I'm going to **veg out** in front of the TV and relax.

Beatrix: Renting videos?

Suzy: And ordering pizza. Andrew and the kids have been **taking turns** cooking meals while I've been working, but tonight we all **get the night off**. Now if I could just decide what to get...

Beatrix: You could try this one—it's really funny.

Suzy: Yeah, I need something **light** and en-tertaining.

Beatrix: The kids've been **bugging me** to rent them this **ninja** movie, but I don't know if I should.

Suzy: It's **pretty** violent. How about this one instead? It's an animal adventure story—thrilling but not too scary.

Beatrix: Great. Thanks.

Words and phrases

1.   What do you think Suzy's workplace has been like if she describes it as a **madhouse**?

2.   The verb **vegetate** means to be physically and mentally inactive, like a vegetable. In informal English, the verb is often shortened to **veg**. The idea of "vegetating" can also be seen in other expressions in English, such as "couch potato," which refers to someone who sits for long periods of time, watching TV or doing some other undemanding activity.

3.   The adjective **light** has many meanings. For example, it can be the opposite of both **heavy** and **dark**. Match each phrase to the best mean-ing of **light**.

light hair	a) lower in fat and calories
light heart	b) less than usual
light punishment	c) not severe
light reading	d) not dark
light sour cream	e) easy to follow
light sleeper	f) easily disturbed
light suitcase	g) with no worries
light use	h) hot heavy

4. "To **bug** someone" is a slang expression. Do you know other words that mean the same thing as **bug**?

Follow-up

1. What is Suzy planning to do? Why?
2. What kind of movies do Suzy and Beatrix want to rent?
3. What kind of movies do you like? Do you like light comedies? Do you like thrillers or suspense movies?

Review it

Read, listen to, and watch some movie reviews. Reviews of **current releases** (movies now showing in theatres) can be found in newspapers and magazines. Video guidebooks evaluate older movies that appear on television or are available on video cassette. In addition, movie critics appear regularly on many television and radio shows.

Prepare your own movie review of a film you have watched recently. Make an oral presentation to your class.

PERSONAL LETTERS

Letter writing was once the only way to communicate with far-away family and friends. Now, most people prefer to talk by telephone.

However, **e-mail** (electronic mail) is making written communication popular again. For example, students get **on-line** services at their college or university, so their parents often **sign up** for an **Internet** account in order to send messages to their children. E-mail messages are different from tradi-

A LETTER TO A FRIEND

December 16, 1996

Dear Yoko,

    Season's greetings! How's life in Yellowknife? I hope that all is going well for you.

    This year has been good for us. It's exciting moving to a new city. We haven't been too **homesick** yet.

    Jean-Luc is doing well at his new job. He enjoys the challenge. The promotion has made the move worthwhile. I thought I would have trouble finding a new job here, but I managed to get an accounting position in a small company close to our house. It's less pressure than my old job, and I have a chance to do more than just **keep the books**.

The move went well. Amazing how much easier it is when the company pays for everything. Remember all those times we moved when we were in university? And the time we moved from Bell St. all by ourselves carrying boxes up and down stairs all night?

The new house is a nice size and it's conveniently located. The **layout** is perfect for us. But the previous owners liked strong colours—we have a lime-green kitchen and a purple bathroom. So, of course, our weekends are spent painting and wallpapering. And we want to start **finishing the basement** as soon as we get some of the decorating done.

The **kids** are settling into their new schools. Zach was excited about starting high school. He's taking instrumental music this year and is playing the clarinet. The sounds coming from his room are starting to sound like real music now. Mandy is in Grade 5. We were lucky that there was a **French immersion** school nearby.

Zach and Mandy are both continuing with their swimming lessons at the local pool. Mandy's also started karate and is enjoying it very much.

This summer we had a family reunion in honour of my great-grandmother's hundredth birthday. Imagine living to be 100! We held it at my cousin's farm in Saskatchewan. There were so many people that we had to put up tents to accommodate them all. We had cousins coming from all over Canada and the States—one even flew over from Germany. I saw relatives whom I hadn't seen  for years, and many whom I met for the very first time.

Hope you have a good holiday. I'll be looking forward to hearing from you and finding out what is new with you and your family. Take care.

Jamie

tional letters. They are usually shorter, are sent more frequently, and are like written conversations.

In contrast to e-mail conversations, annual letters to friends and family are like reports, summarizing the news from the whole year. These letters are often sent at Christmas time.

In personal letters, the style of writing is usually informal. Vocabulary and grammar are more like spoken English than like formal written English.

Words and phrases

1. Compound words with "-sick" include **home-sick**, **carsick**, and **airsick**. How is **homesickness** different from **airsickness**?
2. What do you call someone who **keeps the books** in a company?
3. What does the word **layout** mean? Give examples of different kinds of layouts.
4. What do you do to **finish a basement**?
5. What is **French immersion** schooling?

Follow-up

1. What do you know about Jamie and her family from the letter? For example, how many children does she have and how old are they?
2. Do you think personal letters should be hand-written? What are the advantages of doing letters on a computer?
3. Do you write letters to your family or friends? Do you like writing letters?
4. What kind of experiences have you had moving from one home to another? What was your most difficult move? What was the easiest move you made?

Write it yourself

Write a letter to a friend or relative, someone you haven't been in touch with for a few months.

EARLY RETIREMENT

Erik: So **you guys** been thinking about that early-retirement deal?

Fran: Sure—why not? The cash is **kinda** tempting. Jerry and I have been talking about getting a **condo** down south.

Erik: Sounds good. I don't know what I'd do if I retire, though. My wife's still working, and she's not ready to quit. I'm trying to imagine what I would do at home alone all day.

André: Mm, but there's always volunteer work or a part-time job.

Fran: Yeah, and some people even turn hobbies into jobs after retirement. Ellen does some arrangements for the flower shop occasionally, and Harry works in that old coin shop downtown.

Sophie: I'm **looking forward** to spending more time in my workshop. I like **re-finishing** old furniture. Mostly I just do pieces for the family, but I thought I could sell some.

André: Me, I want to spend some time with my family. My kids live in different parts of the country now, so I'm gonna take turns visiting them—don't **wanna wear out my welcome** in any one spot.

Words and phrases

1. What is **condo** short for? What does it mean?
2. What kind of things are done to **refinish** furniture?

3. Explain the expression **to look forward to** something.

4. How do you **wear out your welcome**?

Follow-up

1. What is Erik thinking about?

2. What are the retirement plans of Fran, Sophie, and André?

3. What are Ellen's and Harry's hobbies?

4. Today, many companies want to reduce their staff, so they offer their employees early-retirement packages. Discuss the advantages and disadvantages of such arrangements for both employers and employees.

5. Discuss retirement. What are the experiences of your friends and relatives? What kind of people adjust well to retirement?

6. Do you have some interests and activities that you could pursue after you retire from your main job? Do you think you would enjoy retirement?

HOUSEWORK

Housework is an important part of everyday life. It can lead to **domestic** arguments—between husbands and wives, between parents and children, and between roommates. Moreover, changes in our society have affected our attitudes towards housework.

With more women working outside the home, household **chores** have become a social issue. Although men spend more time on housework than they did in the past, studies show that women still do **the lion's share** of the work. Men may help with chores, but the work is still considered women's responsibility.

Over the years, technological advances have made housework easier, but the chores have not disappeared. For instance, washing machines and dryers make doing the laundry easier and faster, but we wash our **clothes** more often than our grandmothers did.

Concern for the environment also affects housework. For example, it is important to use less water. Many cleaning products have chemicals (such as chlorine) that are harmful to the environment. Therefore, some people use baking soda and vinegar as **biodegradable** cleaners.

People have different ideas about housework. Some people prefer their surroundings neat and tidy. Other people may keep their rooms very **cluttered**. Some people **don't mind** doing housework. Other people even enjoy it.

Words and phrases

1. What is the difference between **housework** and **homework**?

2. **Lion's share** is an idiom. What do you think it means?

3. **Clothes** is plural. Is there a singular form?

4. Many products are described as **biodegradable**. What does this word mean? What is the prefix and the suffix of this word? What do these parts of the word mean? Check the packaging of products you have around your home to see which ones are biodegradable.

5. What is the difference between a dirty room and a **cluttered** room? Make a list of similar words to describe a room.

Follow-up

1. What does having responsibility for a job mean? How is that different from just helping out?

2. Do you have arguments about housework in your family? What are the main problems?

3. Have you ever lived with a roommate? How did you split the housework? Did you have disagreements over housework?

WOULD YOU MIND?

If you **mind** doing something, you object to doing it or you don't want to do it. (However, **not minding** something does *not* mean that you **like** it, only that you don't **dislike** it.)

> I **don't mind** cooking dinner, but I hate cleaning up afterwards.

> He **doesn't mind** if you call him at work.

Polite requests are often made with the expression **would you mind**?

> Would you mind taking the garbage out?

> *No, I wouldn't mind. (Yes, I will take out the garbage.)*

> Would you mind if I smoked?

> *Yes, I would mind. (I don't want you to smoke.)*

To avoid confusion, the answer is not usually a yes–no answer. For example, you might simply agree to the request by saying "OK" or "all right."

> Would you mind cleaning out the fridge? *OK.*

> Would you mind holding this for me? *All right.*

Notice that **mind** is followed by a gerund (the "ing" form of the verb) and not by the infinitive.

> Do you mind moving your chair over?

> *not* Do you mind to move your chair over?

Ask a classmate to do something using the expression **would you mind?**

HOUSEHOLD CHORES

Look over the list of household chores below. In small groups, discuss the chores.

Which chores are the most difficult?

Which chores do you not mind doing?

Which chores do you like doing?

Which chores would you willingly pay someone to do for you?

How are the household jobs divided in your home? How do you think they should be divided?

Do you think there are some chores that are women's work and some that are men's work?

cooking	dusting
baking	tidying the house
setting the table	sweeping
clearing the table	mopping the floor
doing the dishes	vacuuming
taking the garbage out	gardening
doing the laundry	weeding
ironing	mowing the lawn
mending clothes	repairs and maintenance
sewing	painting and decorating

Find out more

Call a professional house-cleaning agency to find out about rates and services offered. What chores are included in a basic house-cleaning service? What are the "extras" of the deluxe service?

FINDING A ROOMMATE

It can be difficult to find a **compatible roommate**. Sometimes, people who are good friends cannot live together easily.

It is helpful to have similar tastes. For example, if one roommate likes only country music and the other likes only heavy metal, conflict may result.

Of course, roommates don't have to be too much alike. Sometimes it helps to have different talents. For example, one roommate may be a terrific cook and the other might be good at cleaning and repairing.

Think about your lifestyle and daily habits. Make a list of questions to ask a possible roommate. Here are some sample questions:

Do you smoke?

What kind of music do you like? Do you play music often? Do you play it loud?

Are you a morning person or a **night owl**?

Interview your classmates to see who would make a good roommate for you. If you find you are not compatible with someone, change partners until you find a possible roommate.

OWNING A PET

For some people, no house is a home without a pet, and pets are a valued part of the family. Dogs and cats are the most common pets, but some people prefer other animals.

Local governments have laws about pet ownership. For example, the number of cats or dogs kept in a house may be limited. Certain animals, such as chimpanzees or boa constrictors, may not be kept as pets. In addition, some landlords do not allow tenants to have any pets.

LET'S GET A DOG

Kristen: I just saw Mrs. Sobinski walking her new dog. Is he ever cute!

Michael: He's more than just cute, you know. He's one of those specially trained dogs that helps **deaf** people.

Kristen: Really? Like a **seeing-eye dog**?

Michael: Yeah. He's trained to respond to noises—the doorbell, the **smoke detector**...

Kristen: Wow. Well, we don't need a trained dog here. But how about getting a dog as a pet?

Michael: Oh, Kris, we've talked about this before. We agreed that it's just not fair to keep a dog when we're away from home so much.

Kristen: Yeah, but with my new job I'll be working **right around the corner**. I won't have to **commute** and I can even come home for lunch.

Michael: That's true.

Kristen: We could get a **mutt** from the **humane society**. We don't need an expensive **purebred**.

Michael: OK, OK, we'll think about it. Let's just not rush into anything.

Words and phrases

1.   What ability does a **deaf** person lack?

2.   **Mutt** and **purebred** are opposites. Explain the difference. Which is the slang term? **Mongrel** is another word that is used to describe dogs. Is **mongrel** a synonym for **mutt** or **purebred**?

3.   What does the **humane society** do? What does the adjective **humane** mean?

Follow-up

1.   What is special about Mrs. Sobinski's dog? Discuss other ways animals are trained to help people.

2.   How do Michael and Kristen feel about getting a dog? What is Michael worried about?

3.   List the advantages and disadvantages of pets.

4.   Do you have a pet? Tell your classmates about a special pet you had or you knew.

5.   It is said that there are two main kinds of pet lovers: cat people and dog people. Do you prefer cats or dogs? Why?

Find out more

1.   Call or visit your local humane society. Find out more about adopting an animal. For example, how does the society **screen** (choose) potential pet owners? What are the costs involved in getting a pet from the local animal shelter?

2.   Call or visit your city hall to learn more about the local by-laws concerning pets. Which animals cannot be kept as pets? What happens if an animal is considered dangerous? Do you think these laws are good?

STAYING OVERNIGHT

Accommodations for guests vary greatly in Canadian homes. Some people have special guest bedrooms, which may even have **en suite bathrooms**. Sometimes guests sleep on a **sofa bed** in the **den** or family room.

How hosts and guests behave depends on many factors. For example, relatives and close friends might be encouraged to **help themselves** and to **make themselves at home**. They may help out with the meal preparation and the dishes. Guests who are not close to the family may be more formally entertained.

In addition, the type of visit being made is important. If the guests are on a vacation trip, the hosts often plan special activities such as sightseeing. However, the family routine might go on as usual if the guests are staying overnight simply because they need a place to stay.

School-aged children sometimes have **sleep-over** parties for birthdays and other occasions. Sleeping, however, is not the main focus of these activities. A typical scene would be half a dozen 11-year-olds in sleeping-bags in a recreation room watching videos half the night.

Cultural differences can also determine what hosts and guests do. Moreover, people have individual personality differences. Some people are more casual hosts than others.

Words and phrases

1. If your hosts tell you to **help yourself** to something, what do they mean?
2. What do guests do to **make themselves at home**?

Follow-up

1. What do you like and dislike about being an overnight guest? What do you like and dislike about having people stay overnight at your place?
2. What does a good host do? What does a good guest do? Is there a difference between Canadian customs concerning guests and customs in your native culture?

AN OVERNIGHT VISIT

Ian: Bring your bag up and I'll show you your room.

Keith: You know, I really appreciate you and Rebecca **putting me up** like this, especially on such **short notice**.

Ian: No problem—gives us a chance to spend some time together. Since you've been living up north, we hardly get to see you any more.

Keith: Well, if I get this job, you'll be seeing a lot more of me.

Ian: **That'd** be great; I need a new **squash** partner. Here's the **den**—it **doubles as** our guest room. The sofa **pulls out** to make a bed.

Keith: It'll be fine.

Ian: Towels and bedding are in the cupboard. Remind me to leave you a key, since we have to be out of the house before you. Will you be home for dinner?

Keith: Yeah, **I'm supposed to** be done by 3. But how about if I take you and Becky out for dinner? It's the least I can do.

Ian: It's not necessary. But thanks, we'd love to go out.

Words and phrases

1. What does **putting someone up** mean?
2. A **sofa bed** is sometimes called a **pull-out sofa**.

Follow-up

1. Why is Keith staying with Ian and Rebecca?
2. What kind of guest accommodations do Ian and Rebecca have? What arrangements are they making for Keith's visit?
3. Generally, overnight guests bring a gift for their hosts. What could Keith have brought for Ian and Rebecca? What else is he doing to show his appreciation?

TO SUPPOSE

Suppose is a verb that means to believe or to expect. However, when it is used with another verb in the infinitive form, **suppose** is similar to **should**. **Suppose** is used frequently in English and the different meanings can be confusing.

The following sentences illustrate the various meanings of **suppose**.

Suppose is used with the subject **I** to mean think, believe or guess:

> I **suppose** you'll want the day off. (I guess you'll want the day off.)

> I **suppose** you won the race. (I have an idea that you won the race.)

> Are you going to the dance this weekend? I **suppose** so. (I think so, or I might.)

Supposed to can be used with subjects other than **I**. This structure follows the verb **to be** and it needs another verb to complete it:

> I'm **supposed to** show him the factory. (I have been asked to show him the factory.)

> He's **supposed to** be here at six. (He's expected to be here at six. He should be here at six.)

In the past tense, **supposed to** is used for an action that did not happen, even though it was expected.

> I was **supposed to** meet him at 6. (I should have met him at 6, but I didn't.)

> She was **supposed to** drop off the form at the main office. (She should have dropped off the form at the main office, but she didn't.)

Read the following sentences. Decide how **suppose** is being used in the sentence: Does it mean think or believe? Is it used to talk about an expected action? Or, does it show an expected action that did not take place? Explain the meaning of the sentence.

1. They were supposed to wait for us.
2. She's supposed to bring the book with her.
3. I'm supposed to give this form to the supervisor.
4. I suppose you brought your book.
5. I was supposed to go to a meeting, but I forgot.
6. You were supposed to be here earlier.
7. We're supposed to line up over there.
8. I suppose you're ready for the test.

Practise using suppose and supposed to with your classmates.

GUEST ETIQUETTE

It is difficult to know what to do in some social situations. People have different standards of behaviour. **Etiquette** (the rules of polite behaviour) is also different in different cultures.

In small groups, discuss the following situations. What do you do in your home? What do you do as a guest? Think of similar situations you have experienced and discuss them with your classmates.

When you are a guest, do you bring a gift for your host? Discuss suitable gifts for different occasions—a dinner, a party, a weekend visit.

What time do you get up if you are staying overnight in someone else's home? Would you get up before your hosts do?

If you are a non-smoker but your guests smoke, what do you do?

How do you change your normal routine when you have overnight guests?

What should a host provide for overnight guests?

Do you wear shoes inside your home? Do you ask your guests to take off their shoes when they come to your home?

PROVERBS AND SAYINGS

The following proverbs and sayings all speak about the importance of the home. Which proverb do you think says it best?

Home is where the heart is.

Home sweet home.

A man's home is his castle.

East or west, home is best.

There's no place like home.

The importance of family is pointed out in the next proverb. Discuss its meaning.

Blood is thicker than water.

Other proverbs relate to housekeeping. Discuss the idea behind these sayings:

Cleanliness is next to godliness.

A place for everything and everything in its place.

TECHNOLOGY IN THE HOME—PAST, PRESENT, AND FUTURE

Recent technological advances have changed Canadians' lifestyles. Microwave ovens, video cassette recorders (VCRs), and home computers have

all made an impact. What do you think are the most important recent inventions found in the home? Why?

Discuss the advantages and disadvantages of the technological advances that are already being made. For instance, with computer link-ups people can get information from the library, do their banking, and communicate by electronic mail.

In groups, make a technological **wish list**. What kind of inventions could improve our homes? Would you like a robot to clean the floor? Or air cleaners to remove dust? Consider the problems you have at home and how they could be solved.

MORE TO DO

1. What makes a place a home? Discuss your ideas in class and/or write an essay.

2. Visit a sales office for new homes. Look at sample floor plans. What are popular features in modern homes? Pick your favourite house. Why does it suit you?

3. Many cities have "home shows," exhibitions that deal with home products. If possible, visit a home show. Find out what are currently popular products for a house. For example, the home show may have several exhibits of hot tubs, built-in vacuums, or skylights.

On the Road

TRANSPORTATION IN CANADA

Canada is the second largest country in the world. The Trans Canada highway extends 7600 km, from Newfoundland to British Columbia.

Although Canada is a large country, its population is only about 28 million, one-tenth that of the United States. Much of Canada is **uninhabited** and most Canadians live close to the American border. In effect, this population distribution makes Canada a long, narrow country.

Because of Canada's vast size, Canadians have become masters of transportation and communication. The country has been shaped by the railroad: federal politicians promised rail service to both British Columbia and Prince Edward Island in order to persuade them to become provinces of Canada.

Size also explains why Canadians have trouble feeling like they belong to one nation. Most Canadians do not have an opportunity to travel across the entire country and see all the regions of Canada.

Follow-up

1. Why is the geography of Canada important?
2. How long would it take to cross Canada by car or bus? By train? By plane? Make an estimate and then call a travel agency, an automobile association, or the bus or train station to find out how long the typical trip takes.

HOW DO I GET THERE?

Visitor: Excuse me, could you please tell me how to get to Thompson Hall?

Student :   Thompson Hall? Hmmm, is that the engineering building?

Visitor: I think so, but I didn't get much information—just to go to Thompson Hall, Room 101.

Student: Well, if it's the one I think it is, you go down this road a little further and then **hang** a right at the stop sign. It's about half a **block** down—a big **yellowish** building with a lot of windows on the ground floor.

Visitor: Straight down here and right at the stop sign.

Student: That's right. I'm **pretty sure** that's the one. If not, there's a **campus** map there too, so you can check that.

Visitor: Great. Thanks a lot.

Student: **No problem**.

Words and phrases

1. What phrases could replace "I'm **pretty sure**" and "**No problem**" in the dialogue?
2. Define the word **campus**. Describe a campus you are familiar with.

Follow-up

1. Where does this conversation take place?
2. What does the student suggest that the visitor do if the directions are not quite right?
3. Discuss experiences you have had when you were learning to get around an area. Did you have to ask for directions? Were they clear and easy to follow?

GIVING DIRECTIONS

Here are some examples of what people might say when they are giving or receiving directions. Look for important vocabulary in each example. Can you tell how the person is travelling in each example (driving, walking, or taking public transit)?

Go down about three blocks and take a right at the stop lights.

It's about three kilometres down the highway, heading west.

Turn at the corner with the gas station.

Just before Harcourt Street, you'll see a big **billboard** on the left.

Turn right at the street right after you cross the railway tracks.

Take the subway to Finch and then transfer to the westbound 69 bus. Get off at the stop past the courthouse.

So I go straight down here, left at the lights, and left again at the next street? Right?

You can cut across the path there if you want to take a **short cut**.

In groups, make a list of tips or guidelines for giving good directions. (For example, you can tell someone to look for a **landmark**, like a building.) What advice would you give a traveller who has to ask for directions? (For example, how could you avoid being confused by the two meanings of **right**?)

Practise giving directions to your classmates. Give directions to your home and local places of interest. You can bring in maps to help you. You can also take a walk around your school and practise giving directions to different places.

NAMES FOR STREETS

Here are some of the words used with street names in Canadian cities. What is the abbreviation for each?

avenue

boulevard

court

crescent

drive

highway

road

street

City streets have these and other words after their names, but the differences in meaning are not always distinct. Generally, **boulevards** and **drives** are wider and curve more. **Crescents** are U-shaped, curving back to rejoin a street. **Courts** are **dead ends** (they have only one entrance/exit).

However, the use of these terms can vary in different regions. In Edmonton, for example, the roads going north–south are called streets, and those going east–west are called avenues; numbers are used instead of names for each street and avenue.

With a map

Look at a map of your city. Make a list of the words that follow street names, such as "road" and "boulevard." You may find colourful terms such as "lane" or "mews."

Look for any patterns in the street names themselves. For example, all the streets in one area may be named after birds or trees. Sometimes streets are named after famous people.

GETTING A DRIVER'S LICENCE

In small groups, talk about the procedure for getting a driver's licence. Here are some questions:

How old does someone have to be to get a licence?

What is the first step for getting a licence?

Is there a written test of the rules of the road?

How much knowledge of English do you need to get a licence?

Is there a vision test?

What kind of restrictions are there for people who have to wear glasses?

What are the restrictions on beginners' permits?

How long are beginners' permits valid?

What kind of road test is required?

What are the fees for the test and the licence?

How are licences renewed?

Which government department handles drivers' licences?

Where do you call for more information?

　　If you cannot answer some of these questions, or if you are not sure if your information is correct, find out the answers. You can check the driver's handbook for your province or call the local department of transportation office.

FIXING YOUR CAR

Mechanic:	So, what's the problem?
Customer:	I've been having trouble starting the car. The engine **grinds** and **whines** when I **hit the ignition**.
Mechanic:	In the mornings?
Customer:	Yeah, I had to get a **boost** from my neighbour **a couple times**.
Mechanic:	It's been pretty cold the last few weeks. The trouble could be your **battery**. How old's the car?
Customer:	It's **an '88**.
Mechanic:	Hmmm. Well, bring it in and I'll take a look at it.

Words and phrases

1. Describe a **grinding** noise and a **whining** noise.

2. What part of the car is the **ignition**? What is the **battery**?

3. How do you get a **boost** for a car? What piece of equipment is necessary to do this?

4. **A couple times** is an informal, shortened form of **a couple of times**.

Follow-up

1. What is the problem with the customer's car? What does he have to do to get it started?

2. What might be wrong with the car?

3. Are you knowledgeable about cars? Do you think it is important to know something about how a car works? Why or why not?

4. Do you belong to an auto club? What services does it provide?

Make a list

In small groups, make a list of basic automotive vocabulary. Pick words that are useful for everyone, including those who know very little about machines. Include words such as **accelerator**, **brake**, **muffler**, and **windshield**. Use reference books such as automotive manuals, if necessary.

DRIVING LESSONS

In groups, discuss the vocabulary in the phrases below. Then, pretend that you are giving instructions to someone who is behind the wheel of a car for the first time, and put the instructions in their proper order.

Put the key in the ignition.

Buckle your seatbelt.

Check the rear-view mirror.

Check the side mirrors.

Turn the key.

Put your foot on the brake.

Back the car out of the parking space.

Put the car in reverse.

Release the emergency brake.

Turn on the headlights.

Put your foot on the accelerator.

What other instructions would you give during a driving lesson?

VEHICLES FOR SALE

What kind of vehicle do you prefer? Discuss the advantages of the different kinds.

sedan	mini-van
compact car	van
luxury car	truck
sports car	motorcycle
station wagon	bicycle

PREPOSITIONS

Talking about travel and transportation requires the use of prepositions such as "on" and "by."

Fill in the blanks with prepositions (*by, in, on, with*) and/or articles (*a, an, the*) to make the sentences grammatically correct.

1. I go to school _____ bus.

2. I go to work _____ foot.

3. I try to travel _____ bike whenever I can, but sometimes I take public transit.

4. The best way to get there is _____ train.

5. To use the car pool lane, you have to have at least three people _____ car.

6. I always read when I'm sitting _____ subway.

7. When I'm riding _____ my bike, I feel free and happy.

8. While I was riding _____ bus, I saw him walking down the street.

9. Going _____ plane is fastest.

What colour of car do you like (interior and exterior colour)?

If you own a car, describe it to your classmates.

Read some ads for used cars from the newspaper. What are the important details that a used-car buyer needs to know?

PUBLIC TRANSPORTATION

Use the vocabulary in the list below to fill in the blanks in the passage.

commuters

drop-off point

exact fare

LRTs

passes

route

seeing someone off

token

transfer

turnstile

To ride on the transit system, you may use a **ticket** or pay cash. However, if bus drivers do not make change, the _____ is required. Sometimes you can purchase weekly, monthly, or annual bus _____ .

Buses follow a particular _____ , and if you have to change buses when you travel, you ask for a _____ , a piece of paper marked with the time, date, and route travelled.

When you travel by bus, you pay your **fare** by dropping it into the box next to the driver. In a subway, you might pay at the cashier or use a _____ and pass through a _____ . In addition to buses and subways, some city transit systems use **streetcars** and _____ (light rail transportation).

Some transit systems use trains to bring _____ from the suburbs into the downtown core. One colourful term is the "kiss 'n ride," a _____ for people taking the transit system. The name refers to the act of _____ with a goodbye kiss.

Follow-up

1. What do you think about the public transit system in your area? Is it convenient? Is it reasonably priced? Do you use the system regularly?

2. Explain to a classmate how to get to your home using public transit.

A RADIO CALL-IN SHOW

Jane: This is Talk Radio—your chance to **air** your **beefs**. Today we're talking about driving in Toronto. What do you think is the worst **hazard** on the roads? Arshi from Scarborough, go ahead, you're **on the air**.

Arshi: Hello, Jane. I just want to say that I **can't stand** those guys who **zip** into any little space they can find in between cars on the 401. I try to keep enough space in front of me for safe stopping, and then some idiot squeezes in there, **cutting me off**.

Jane: And when they're not **weaving**, they're **tailgating**.

Arshi: Yeah, they figure they can save a few seconds by squeezing past every car. It's just not worth it, though.

Jane: Absolutely. So, all you listeners out there, remember to keep a safe **brak-**

ing distance between you and the car ahead. Next caller...Harry, what's your beef?

Harry: Let's face it: winter is the worst hazard of all—freezing rain, **black ice**, **drifting snow**, and those **potholes** the ice leaves behind.

Jane: Mmm. And then, when spring comes, you have all the slow-downs from the construction crews fixing those potholes. Let's hear from our next caller, Bill, who's calling from a car phone on the 401.

Bill: Hi, Jane. I can't stand **rubbernecking**. There's an accident somewhere and, before you know it, everybody has to slow down to take a look. Traffic slows to a **crawl** even when the accident isn't blocking a lane.

Jane: You wouldn't happen to be in one of those **traffic jams** right now, would you?

Bill: How'd you guess?

Words and phrases

Match each word in the list with the correct definition.

air (*verb*)	hazard
beef	potholes
black ice	rubbernecking
can't stand something	tailgating
crawling	traffic jams
cut someone off	weave
drifting snow	zip

a) complaint

b) danger

c) broadcast, put on radio or television

d) move quickly to another spot

e) move in front of someone, interfere in his or her path

f) cars blocked on the road

g) change lanes often to pass cars

h) following another car too closely

i) frozen, slippery spots on the road that are difficult to see

j) holes in the road formed by ice damage

k) looking at an accident as you pass the scene

l) moving forward slowly

m) dislike, be unable to tolerate something

n) snow that blows across the road, making it difficult to see

Which words and expressions are informal or slang?

Follow-up

1. In your own words, explain each caller's complaint.

2. What do you think of the complaints voiced on the radio talk show? Can you think of solutions to the problems?

3. If you were a caller, what would you complain about? Discuss the road problems you've seen.

4. Choose one of the following topics and role-play a radio talk show. One or two students can act as hosts. The other students can be "callers."

   • how to encourage people to take public transit

   • how to improve transportation in your city or region

   • how to make the roads safer

   • how to improve air travel

If you wish, your talk show could be about something other than transportation. You might want to have a talk show about one of the other issues you have discussed in class.

Listen in

Radio talk shows are popular in Canada. Callers phone in to give their opinions on different subjects. The hosts of such shows often have special guests, who are experts on the topic, to help answer the calls.

List the major radio stations in your city or region. Find out when talk shows are scheduled. Listen to three different talk shows in one week. Make a list of the issues discussed, the names of the hosts, and the names of guest experts. Which talk show did you like the best? Report to the class on your findings.

AN ACCIDENT REPORT

I was driving southbound along Riverside Drive in the left-hand lane. It was raining lightly and the road was slippery. I saw this kid **dash** across the street in front of me. I **slammed on the brakes**, the car **skidded**, and I bumped into the car travelling in the lane beside me. That driver seemed to be braking as well. Both of us came to a stop at the side of the road. The kid who had run across the road **ran off**.

Words and phrases

1. **Dash** and **run off** both describe running actions. How are these actions different?

2. **Slam** describes a hard, almost violent action. Can you think of other things that are slammed?

3. Describe what happens when a car **skids**.

Follow-up

1. In your own words, explain what happened in this accident.

2. Have you ever had a car accident? What happened?

3. The police collect written statements from all the people involved in an accident and from the witnesses. Write the accident report that the other driver might have written. Or write a report from one of the witnesses' point of view.

4. Write a report on an event that occurred recently. The event can be something that you witnessed or something that happened to you. It can be an accident, a crime, or any event that had a lot of action.

Find it out

What should you do when you have a car accident? Find out what the police advise. For example, for small accidents (informally called **fender benders**) you might not have to wait for the police to arrive; you just get insurance information from the other driver.

Guidelines are published in the driver's handbook for your province, but you might have to call the police for more complete information.

PLANNING A VACATION TRIP

Patrick: I've got a couple of weeks off this August. **What say** we load the kids in the car and head east?

Kate: Really? Go to the **Maritimes**? Can we afford it?

Patrick: We might have to **cut some corners** on accommodations, but we can manage, I think.

Kate: Yeah, we could stay in **bed and breakfasts** or even take the tent and camp out.

Patrick: Sure. And the universities offer cheap rooms in their residences, you know.

Kate: I know Amy has been **dying** to go to P.E.I. ever since she read *Anne of Green Gables*.

Patrick: And the kids will have all sorts of forts and **historical sites** on the **itinerary**.

Kate: I know. The fortress at Louisbourg, the Canadian Naval Museum...

Patrick: Sounds great. This trip'll be educational and fun.

Words and phrases

1. What provinces are included in the **Maritimes**? Are the Atlantic provinces the same as the Maritimes?

2. What does **cut corners** mean? Give examples.

3. **Bed and breakfast** is an expression used as a unit to describe a place. Note the plural form in the dialogue. How is a bed and breakfast different from other vacation accommodations?

4. *Anne of Green Gables* is a famous Canadian novel written by Lucy Maud Montgomery in 1908. What is the story about?

Follow-up

1. Where does this family probably live?

2. What are they planning to do on their vacation?

3. What are some ways for families to cut costs while travelling?

4. Where would you like to go if you were planning a trip within Canada? What would you like to see there?

5. Research tourist attractions in the Maritimes. Find out about the Fortress of Louisbourg, the Canadian Naval Museum, and the Anne of Green Gables house.

HUMAN LOCOMOTION

Moving around on two feet is an important method of transportation. Many different verbs refer to human locomotion, such as **walk**, **run**, and **skip**. The words describe different kinds of movement.

From the list of words below, fill in the blanks in the sentences. Some of the words can be nouns as well as verbs. (You may have to change the form of the word slightly; for example, you may have to add a verb ending.)

dash

glide

hike

jog

march

skip

stroll

toddle

trudge

wander

1. It was such a nice day that we decided to _____ in the park.

2. My nephew is learning to walk. It's so funny to watch him _____ across the living-room.

3. The soldiers _____ onto the parade grounds.

4. After work, I like to put on my running gear and go _____ in the park.

5. I got lost in that neighbourhood and I _____ around for a long time before I recognized some landmarks.

6. Let's go out to the countryside this weekend. We can go _____ in the hills.

7. After a full day of shopping, I _____ home exhausted.

8. I saw the bus coming, so I had to _____ across the road to get to the stop on time.

9. The little girls were playing. They _____ down the street hand in hand.

10. In dance class, I learned to _____ across the floor gracefully.

CANADIANS AND THE COTTAGE

Many Canadians enjoy going to a **cottage** during the summer. Cottages are often on a lake or river. Some people own their own summer homes. Others rent a cottage for a week or two. In some parts of Canada, cottages are called **camps**.

Cottages may be small cabins with no plumbing or electricity. However, some cottages are large, fully equipped houses. Some cottages are **winterized** and used for vacations all year.

GOING TO THE COTTAGE

Emily: I'm going up to my brother's cottage this weekend. Want to come along?

Winnie: A cottage? Hmm, I don't know about that.

Emily: C'mon, it'll be great. We can hike, swim, and go canoeing.

Winnie: You know me. I'm a city person. Isn't this the cottage with no indoor plumbing?

Emily: Using the **outhouse** isn't so bad.

Winnie: And no electricity? No television? What would we do in the evenings?

Emily: We have gas lamps for light, and cards and board games for entertainment. Don't be such a **wimp**. We'll have lots of fun.

Words and phrases

1. The suffix "-ize" makes verbs out of nouns. What does **winterize** mean? Here are some other examples: economize, computerize, victimize, dramatize.

2. **Wimp** is a slang term used to criticize someone. Based on the dialogue, what kind of person does this term describe?

Follow-up

1. Why does Emily want to go to the cottage?

2. Why is Winnie hesitating?

3. Would you like to go to this cottage? Why or why not? Are you a city person or a country person?

4. What are your favourite board games? Do you enjoy playing cards? Do you like party games, such as charades? Make a list of entertainment activities that do not require electricity.

MORE TO DO

1. Pick up a driver's handbook in English from the local provincial transportation department and bring it to class. In small groups, make a list of useful vocabulary: for example, expressions about driving include parallel parking, one-way street, and U-turn.

2. You don't have to travel to be a tourist. Make a list of tourist attractions in your area. Include museums, galleries, zoos, and historical sites.

   Many tourist attractions have recorded messages giving general information. Call and listen to a message for one place. Make a note of opening hours, location, admission prices, and special events. Bring the information you find to class and check your listening comprehension.

3. Prepare an oral presentation for the class on a travel and tourism topic. You can talk about an adventure you had while travelling, or you might describe a place you visited.

Answer Keys

UNIT 1: AT SCHOOL

Starting School

1. "She just turned five" means she recently had her fifth birthday.

Registration Requirements

Registering for school may require several steps. First, you choose your program by looking in the school <u>calendar</u>. This booklet gives course descriptions, timetables, and other important information.

Sometimes <u>counsellors</u> help you choose your courses. You may have to meet certain conditions to take a course. For example, some classes may have <u>prerequisite</u> courses, such as introductory courses. Sometimes special arrangements have to be made and you must get the professor's permission. For courses that require a certain level of skill, such as language classes, students may have to write a <u>placement test</u> before registering. These tests help teachers <u>evaluate</u> your level.

When you choose your courses, you also <u>fill out</u> a registration form and pay <u>tuition</u> fees.

Signing up for an English Course

Register and **sign up** mean the same thing. **Sign up** is a phrasal verb and is less formal.

Spending Time on Time

1. Do you <u>have</u> a minute? I'd like to talk to you now.

2. I've never really <u>spent</u> any time with her, so I don't know her very well.

3. <u>Take</u> your time. You don't have to rush.

4. <u>Give</u> me a minute. I'm not ready yet.

5. This watch doesn't <u>keep</u> good time. I'm often late for my appointments.

6. We walked around the mall because we had some time to <u>kill</u> before the movie started.

7. Janice says she's very busy, but I think that if she really wanted to see us, she'd <u>make</u> time.

8. I don't really like to <u>take/spend</u> any more time on housework than the absolute minimum.

9. I have to hurry. I don't have a second to <u>waste/spare.</u>

10. Time seems to <u>pass</u> so slowly when I'm in class.

Phrasal Verbs

I had a bad day at school. It got off to a bad start when I <u>got up</u> late. I'd been <u>looking forward to</u> the field trip that was planned, but then I discovered that the bus had <u>broken down</u> and the field trip <u>was called off</u>. So we ended up having the regular schedule and I hadn't done my math homework. I even <u>left</u> my notebook <u>behind</u> and I had to <u>take down</u> my notes on a scrap piece of paper. Then, in chemistry lab, my Bunsen burner <u>blew up</u>. Luckily, no one was close by at the time and the teacher <u>put</u> the fire <u>out</u> quickly. My brother had promised to give me a ride home, but he forgot to <u>pick me up</u> and I had to take the bus.

Their First University Lecture

gonna = going to

psych = psychology

T.A. = teaching assistant

geez = gee whiz

A Parent–Teacher Interview

1. take a seat, sit down

2. Synonyms for **uneasy** include worried, troubled, anxious, and uncomfortable.

3. "Above grade level" means better than is usually expected of a child in that grade.

Notes to the Teacher

1. **Convenient** is the opposite of **inconvenient**. **Inconvenient** is an adjective. The noun form is **inconvenience**, as in "Sorry for the inconvenience."

2. Students take a **midterm** halfway through a course to show what they have learned so far.

   Students take a **make-up test** if they miss a scheduled test. It is also known as a "supplemental test."

   The **final exam** is the most important test, taken at the end of a course.

For an **open-book exam**, students can refer to their textbook and notes.

A **pop quiz** is a small test, given with no advance warning.

UNIT 2: IN THE COMMUNITY

Ask the Librarian

1. An **annual report** tells a company's stockholders how the business has done over the year.

2. A **directory** is a book with a list of names or facts arranged in alphabetical order. The telephone book is the most common example of a directory.

3. **High tech** is short for **high technology**. The opposite is **low tech**. Computers are high-tech; pen and paper is low-tech.

Library Words and Expressions

When you need to find a book in the library, you consult the catalogue. Books are listed by author, title, and subject. Libraries may record their books on cards, in microfilm records, or in computers.

When you find the record of the book you want, it is important to take a note of the call number, which is a series of numbers and letters that tells you where the book is on the shelves.

If you need help finding the information you need, you ask the librarian at the reference desk.

Some books in the library do not **circulate** (you cannot borrow them). These books are reference books such as dictionaries and encyclopedias. You can use them in the library to look up the information you need.

After you have selected the books you wish to borrow, you take them to the circulation desk. If the library is computerized, the librarian uses a scanner to read the bar code on your library card and on each of the books.

When you borrow books, you should check the due date to know when you have to return the books. You have to pay **fines** on overdue (late) books.

Check It Out

1. Check-out time in the hotel is 11 a.m., so make sure you get everything packed up early.

2. The airline recommends getting to the airport an hour before the flight so that you have time to check in.

3. The check-out lines at the supermarket are always very long.

4. She'll be going to the University of Waterloo in the fall, so she's gone down to check out the campus, the residences, and the city.

5. Check it out! I just bought this new CD.

Swimming Lessons

1. **Aquatics** includes swimming, diving, water skiing, and water polo.

2. **Rec** is short for **recreation**.

Fears

Nouns: fear, fright

Verbs: fear, scare, frighten

Adjectives: frightened, scared, frightening, scary, afraid

He Shoots! He Scores?

breakaway: b) when a player has a clear way to the goal, with no defensive players blocking

deke: d) a move where a player makes a fake shot or movement to draw a defending player out of position

save: a) when a goalie stops the puck from entering the net

ticked off: c) upset or angry

A Letter to the Editor

1. You could say "stop," "cancel," or "eliminate."

The Long and the Short of It

1. broad-minded: h) willing to accept new ideas
2. far-sighted: c) needing glasses to see things close up
3. long-winded: g) talking a long time without stopping
4. narrow-minded: e) not accepting other points of view
5. near-sighted: b) needing glasses to see things far away, only able to see up close
6. short-handed: a) lacking staff
7. short-lived: d) not lasting a long time
8. short-tempered: f) quick to get angry

Garage Sales

Garage sales have become very popular in Canada. People want to <u>recycle</u> things they no longer need, instead of throwing more into the garbage. In addition, people can save money by buying <u>second-hand</u> goods.

Items sold at garage sales vary. You can buy clothing, toys, books, kitchen wares, and home decorations. Because children <u>outgrow</u> clothes and toys so quickly, you will find a lot of these items for sale. Sometimes you find <u>brand-new</u> things: people may sell something they received as a gift and never used, or people who have their own **retail** business may sell off <u>surplus</u> goods at their garage sales.

Usually, items sold at garage sales are priced very cheaply. In fact, many things can be bought for less than a dollar. People often try to <u>bargain</u>, offering a lower price.

Since goods are usually displayed outdoors, garage sales are sometimes called <u>yard sales</u>. A <u>moving sale</u> occurs when people wish to sell their furniture and household items before they move; these sales may be inside the house.

Second-hand goods are also sold by charities or as a business. Sometimes churches and community groups hold <u>rummage sales</u>; people in the community donate the things that are sold, and the money is used for charity. Professional dealers may organize **flea markets**. <u>Auctions</u> are professionally organized also, but in these events the buyers must **bid** for the goods.

Three words that are used instead of "things" are **goods**, **items**, and **wares**.

Let's Have a Garage Sale

1. Spring cleaning is a thorough, rather than just a surface, cleaning, and is performed much less often. Spring cleaning involves such chores as washing walls, rearranging closets, and getting rid of unwanted items.
2. Other slang terms for money include **dough**, **bread**, and **moola**.

Contractions and "Have Got"

Main verbs are marked in italics.

1. I **would** rather *see* the movie downtown.
2. He **will** be *taking* the train this time.
3. They **have** *been* to Vancouver before.
4. She **is** *taking* the seven o'clock flight.
5. I *am* sure that it **will not** take much time.
6. She *is* a lawyer.
7. Marie **is** *going* to Newfoundland for a holiday.
8. You *are* sure you *want* to go tomorrow?
9. I should **have** *taken* the train instead.
10. They **are** *buying* a new house.

UNIT 3: AT THE MALL

The Mall as Community Centre

You can watch a movie in a cinema, attend a lecture in an auditorium, borrow a book in a library, ride a carousel in an amusement park, report a crime in a police station, and go skating at a rink. Someone can take care of your children in a daycare centre. You can have your teeth fixed in a dentist's office or have your will drawn up in a lawyer's office.

Buying a Dream

addictive: d) causing a habit that is hard to break

afford: j) have enough money to buy something

controversial: b) causing disagreement, argument or debate

daydream: h) imagine pleasant ideas of how your life could be

every now and then: a) occasionally, once in a while

hang on: f) wait (informal)

having your head in the clouds: c) always dreaming, unrealistic, not practical

immoral: e) not right, not good, going against principles

realist: i) practical person, not a dreamer

sec: g) a short period of time, a second (shortened form, informal)

Hanging Around with "Hang"

1. I tried to explain the problem on the phone, but he just <u>hung up</u>. He still won't talk to me.

2. She's trying to teach me the butterfly stroke in swimming class, but I just can't <u>get the hang of it</u>.

3. You can <u>hang/hang up</u> your jacket on that rack.

4. She told me to <u>hang on</u> while she looked for the right report.

5. I'm worried about my son. I don't like the kids he's been <u>hanging around with</u> lately.

6. At the first set of lights, <u>hang a right/left</u> at Browning Street.

7. Oops, I've got another call coming in. Can you just <u>hang on</u> a second while I check if it's the call I've been waiting for?

Banking Terms

If you want to use banking services, first you have to open an <u>account</u>. Generally, you do your banking at one <u>branch</u> of the bank, usually a location near your home or your work.

When you make your transactions in the bank, you deal with the <u>tellers</u>. These people give you money when you make a <u>withdrawal</u> from your account or take your money when you make a <u>deposit</u>. If you have chequing and savings accounts, you might have to <u>transfer funds</u> between accounts.

Some people prefer to do their banking electronically or by telephone. When you sign up to use the bank machine service, you are given a card and an <u>access code</u>, which is your secret identification number.

Bank machines have different names. Your bank might call it an ATM (Automatic Teller Machine) or an ABM (Automatic Bank Machine). In everyday speech, people use the general term "bank machine" or they use the brand name of their bank's ATM.

For example, they might say, "I need to go to the Instabank" or "I'm looking for the Green Machine."

In addition to the everyday transactions, you may deal with other bank officers to arrange <u>loans</u>, make investments, rent a safety deposit box, and use other banking services.

Using a Bank Machine

1. queue

2. to screw something up = to make a mistake

to give something a shot = to try to do something

Eating at the Food Court

1. **Stir-frying** requires little fat. Food is stirred often to prevent sticking and to cook the food thoroughly. In **deep-frying**, the food is immersed in hot oil.

2. The fish is dipped in batter and deep-fried. Potatoes are cut in long pieces and deep-fried to make French fries, which are called **chips** in Canada and in England.

Going to the Dentist

"For ages" means "for a very long time." Other expressions include "forever," "for an eternity."

Words for the Dentist's Office

1. When we are about six years old, we start losing our <u>baby teeth</u>.

2. The <u>dental hygienist</u> cleans your teeth and gives them a **fluoride treatment** to help prevent **decay**.

3. When I was a teenager, I had to wear ugly metal <u>braces</u>, but I guess it was worth it now.

4. My tooth has to be **capped** with a <u>crown</u>.

5. I hate getting **fillings**. The **drill** doesn't bother me, but I don't like getting needles for <u>freezing</u> my mouth.

6. The back teeth are called <u>molars</u>.

7. I just had a dental **check-up**—no <u>cavities</u>!

8. I have such a terrible <u>toothache</u>.

9. Young adults often get new molars, but these <u>wisdom teeth</u> sometimes get **pulled**.

Marketing in Grocery Stores

When you go to a grocery store, you enter a world that has been carefully arranged to encourage you to make <u>impulse</u> purchases and spend more money than you planned.

As you approach the store, you may smell the enticing <u>aroma</u> of fresh baked bread. Near the entrances you will usually see displays of fresh fruit and vegetables or a deli and meat counter, because fresh food is more attractive than <u>packaged</u>, prepared foods.

As you push your cart up and down the <u>aisles</u>, you notice the more expensive brands of foods at your eye-level. Cheaper brands are usually at the bottom of the shelf.

The <u>pricing</u> of items is also significant. $2.99 seems a lot cheaper than $3.00. When items are priced at 3 for 99 cents, you are <u>likely</u> to buy three even if you only need one.

The names of products and the design of packaging are carefully chosen to <u>appeal</u> to consumers. Cleaning products, for example, have short, strong names. Laundry detergent is found in green, blue, or yellow boxes. Foods have **homey**, personal names (like Mrs. Brown's Soup) to make you think of home-cooking.

Near the <u>checkout</u>, you see racks full of magazines and candy; both are small, inexpensive items that people are likely to buy on impulse.

Generic and Brand Names

Aspirin = ASA (Acetylsalicylic acid)

Coke = cola

Jello = gelatin

Rollerblades = in-line skates

Saran Wrap = plastic wrap

Scotch tape = clear tape, transparent tape

Skidoo = snowmobile

Styrofoam = plastic foam, polystyrene

Thermos = vacuum bottle

UNIT 4: AT WORK

Starting a Small Business

comes in handy: c) becomes useful (informal)

go belly-up: h) go out of business, die (slang)

landscaping: b) arranging trees, shrubs, and flowers in an area to make a pleasing appearance

liquidated: f) sold to get quick cash

nursery: a) place where plants and trees are grown and sold; also a place for children

pink slip: d) the notice employees receive when they are fired or laid-off from a job

start-up costs: g) expenses of beginning a business

tough: e) difficult, hard (informal)

Calling in Sick

1. In English, you **catch** a cold and other diseases, like the flu. You can also catch a ball, a train, or a show.

2. **Bug** means a mild illness like a cold or flu.

3. The signs of a fever include a hot forehead, flushed cheeks, and glassy eyes.

These expressions mean that the person might have a fever:

I've got a temperature.

She looks flushed.

Her forehead's hot.

"He's shivering so much his teeth are chattering" means that he has a chill. Chills can accompany a fever, but do not show someone feels hot.

"He gets hot under the collar easily" means that he gets angry easily.

Talking about Your Aches and Pains

1. I have to make an appointment with the dentist. I have a <u>toothache</u>.

2. After the car accident, I had a constant <u>backache</u>. It made it difficult to sit for long periods of time.

3. You should wash your hands often so you don't spread <u>germs</u>.

4. The professor had to cancel class because he had <u>laryngitis</u> and couldn't talk.

5. His cold affected his lungs and he had a loud <u>cough</u> for weeks afterwards.

6. I'm allergic to cats. Cat hair makes me <u>sneeze</u>.

7. When you go to the doctor, he asks about your <u>symptoms</u>. Then he tells you what is wrong with you.

8. She had the <u>chills</u> so bad that she was shivering and her teeth were chattering.

No Smoking in the Workplace

1. The reference could be to "the latest news."
2. Someone would say they are going to "have a cigarette."
3. Dennis could have said "That won't work" or "That's not a good idea."

Adverbs at Work

accurately: a) carefully and exactly with good attention to detail; making no mistakes

efficiently: g) well; without wasting time or effort

enthusiastically: b) eagerly; with strong interest

indifferently: d) not caring about the result

industriously: h) working hard, with a lot of effort

methodically: f) using an ordered system

promptly: e) right away; without waiting

sloppily: c) making careless mistakes

The New Employee

1. "**Figures**" is a shortened form of "It figures." It means that the person is not surprised to hear the news, that he expected it, that it makes sense.
2. **Gadgets** include kitchen utensils like peelers and zesters. You can also refer to small electrical appliances like pencil-sharpeners and letter-openers as gadgets.

Computer Talk

Computers have changed both the workplace and the English language. New words about computers enter the vocabulary faster than dictionaries can keep up with them. Some of this vocabulary is highly technical, but much of it becomes part of the everyday language. Computers are so important that everyone talks about the need to be <u>computer literate</u>, or knowledgeable about computers.

The pieces of equipment that make up a computer are called <u>hardware</u>. A computer also needs **software**—electronic instructions called <u>programs</u>.

What used to be called **typing** is now called <u>key-</u>

<u>boarding</u> and **word processing**. <u>Desktop publishing</u> includes arranging the words on the page in an attractive **layout** and using computer-generated pictures (<u>graphics</u>) and different print styles (<u>fonts</u>).

Word processing is one of the most popular uses of a computer. In addition, financial statements can be prepared on a computer using a <u>spreadsheet</u>, which has columns and rows of numbers. <u>Databases</u> are programs that store information such as client files. You can find specific files and sort them in different ways.

Comments by E-mail

1. In the dialogue, **draft** refers to "an early version of a piece of writing."
2. **Editing** includes correcting spelling and grammar mistakes, deleting unnecessary words, and clarifying meaning.
3. **Jargon** is words and expressions common to a particular field. For example, doctors use medical jargon. If people who are not specialists in a certain field read a document, they will not understand it if there is too much jargon.

A Promotion!

Examples of slang:

He **got canned** because he had a bad attitude.

One-third of that department will be getting **pink slips**.

If she comes in late once more, she'll **get sacked**.

UNIT 5: AT HOME

A Weekend at Home

3. light hair: d) not dark

   light heart: g) with no worries

   light punishment: c) not severe

   light reading: e) easy to follow

   light sour cream: a) lower in fat and calories

   light sleeper: f) easily disturbed

   light suitcase: h) not heavy

   light use: b) less than usual

4. bug = annoy, bother, irritate

A Letter to a Friend

1. If you are **airsick**, you are sick because you are in the air. If you are **homesick**, you are sick because you miss your home. Airsickness is a physical ailment, but homesickness is primarily emotional.

2. bookkeeper

3. **Layout** means the way something is arranged. For example, the layout of a house is shown in a floor plan. The layout of a book is the manner in which the words and pictures are arranged.

4. **Finishing a basement** includes insulating, putting up walls, wiring, installing a ceiling, and putting in flooring.

5. In **French immersion**, English-speaking children attend classes with a French-speaking teacher who speaks only French to the children.

Early Retirement

1. **Condo** is short for **condominium**, which is a unit in an apartment which is owned, not rented.

2. To **refinish** furniture, the old finish is stripped off, often with chemicals. The furniture is sanded, and a new finish, such as paint or varnish, is applied.

3. If you **look forward to** something, you are waiting for something pleasurable to happen.

4. You **wear out your welcome** if you stay too long or do something that makes your host not want you to stay any longer.

Housework

1. **Housework** refers to the chores that people do to keep a house clean. **Homework** is school work assigned to be completed at home.

2. The **lion's share** is the majority or the larger part of something.

3. **Cloth** refers to the material from which clothes are made. The only singular for **clothes** would be "a piece of clothing."

4. **Biodegradable** materials decompose naturally. The prefix **bio** refers to life. For example,

biology is the study of life forms. The suffix **able** refers to an ability. Therefore, **biodegradable** means that something is able to degrade (decompose) by the action of living organisms such as insects and bacteria.

5. A **cluttered** room has many objects inside it, but it may be quite clean. A synonym is **messy**. Words that mean the opposite are **neat** and **tidy**.

Let's Get a Dog

1. A **deaf** person cannot hear.

2. **Mutt** is a slang word for a dog that is mixed breed, and **mongrel** is a synonym. A **purebred** dog is recognizable as one breed of dog, like a German shepherd.

3. The **humane society** takes care of unwanted pets. **Humane** is related to the word **human** and means "in a civilized, kind way."

Staying Overnight

1. You **help yourself** by serving yourself, by taking some food or drink from what is offered.

2. Guests who **make themselves at home** behave less formally than other guests do. For example, a guest who makes herself at home will serve herself a glass of water, without waiting to be offered some.

An Overnight Visit

1. If you **put someone up**, you let him or her stay overnight at your home.

To Suppose

The sentences are explained here using other words, to show the meaning.

1. They were supposed to wait for us.

   We expected them to wait, but they didn't.

2. She's supposed to bring the book with her.

   She should bring her book. She was told to bring her book.

3. I'm supposed to give this form to the supervisor.

   I was told to give this form to the supervisor.

4. I suppose you brought your book.

    I guess that you brought your book.

5. I was supposed to go to a meeting, but I forgot.

    I should have gone to the meeting, but I didn't.

6. You were supposed to be here earlier.

    We expected you to be here earlier, but you are late.

7. We're supposed to line up over there.

    We should line up over there.

    Someone told us to line up over there.

8. I suppose you're ready for the test.

    I expect you are ready for the test.

UNIT 6: ON THE ROAD

How Do I Get There?

1. Someone could say "I think so" or "I'm almost certain" instead of "I'm pretty sure." The student could have answered "You're welcome" instead of saying "No problem."

2. A **campus** is the grounds and buildings of a multi-building school, like a college or university.

Names for Streets

avenue = Ave.

boulevard = Blvd.

court = Ct.

crescent = Cr. or Cres.

drive = Dr.

highway = Hwy

road = Rd.

street = St.

Fixing Your Car

1. A blender makes a grinding noise. A whining noise is high and sharp.

2. The ignition is where you put the key to start the car. The battery keeps an electrical charge to start the engine.

3. You get a boost from another person's car.

Booster cables are attached from the battery of one car to the battery of the other.

Prepositions

1. I go to school <u>by</u> bus.

2. I go to work <u>on</u> foot.

3. I try to travel <u>by</u> bike whenever I can, but sometimes I take public transit.

4. The best way to get there is <u>by/on the</u> train.

5. To use the car pool lane, you have to have at least three people <u>in the</u> car.

6. I always read when I'm sitting <u>on the</u> subway.

7. When I'm riding (<u>on</u>) my bike, I feel free and happy. (The preposition "on" can be omitted here.)

8. While I was riding <u>the/on the</u> bus, I saw him walking down the street.

9. Going <u>by</u> plane is fastest.

Public Transportation

To ride on the transit system, you may use a **ticket** or pay cash. However, if bus drivers do not make change, the <u>exact fare</u> is required. Sometimes you can purchase weekly, monthly, or annual bus <u>passes</u>.

Buses follow a particular <u>route</u>, and if you have to change buses when you travel, you ask for a <u>transfer</u>, a piece of paper marked with the time, date, and route travelled.

When you travel by bus, you pay your **fare** by dropping it into the box next to the driver. In a subway, you might pay at the cashier or use a <u>token</u> and pass through a <u>turnstile</u>. In addition to buses and subways, some city transit systems use **streetcars** and <u>LRTs</u> (light rail transportation).

Some transit systems use trains to bring <u>commuters</u> from the suburbs into the downtown core. One colourful term is the "kiss 'n ride," a <u>drop-off point</u> for people taking the transit system. The name refers to the act of <u>seeing someone off</u> with a goodbye kiss.

A Radio Call-in Show

air: c) broadcast, put on radio or television

beef: a) complaint (slang)

black ice: i) frozen, slippery spots on the road that are difficult to see

can't stand something: m) dislike, be unable to tolerate something (informal)

crawling: l) moving forward slowly

cut someone off: e) move in front of someone, interfere in his or her path

drifting snow: n) snow that blows across the road, making it difficult to see

hazard: b) danger

potholes: j) holes in the road formed by ice damage

rubbernecking: k) looking at an accident as you pass the scene (slang)

tailgating: h) following another car too closely

traffic jams: f) cars blocked on the road

weave: g) change lanes often to pass cars

zip: d) move quickly to another spot (informal)

An Accident Report

1. **Dash** means a quick and sudden movement, whereas **run off** just means to leave the scene.

2. Doors are slammed. A book can be slammed on to a desk.

3. When a wheel skids, it locks so it can't turn. The car slides.

Planning a Vacation Trip

1. The **Maritimes** are Nova Scotia, New Brunswick, and Prince Edward Island. Newfoundland is an Atlantic province, but it is not in the Maritimes.

2. **Cut corners** means to save money by not doing some things or by reducing things. For example, you can cut corners at a party by having snacks instead of a meal.

3. A **bed and breakfast** is usually in a house rather than a motel or hotel. Guests often have to share a bathroom. Accommodations are cheaper, and breakfast is included in the price.

4. *Anne of Green Gables* is about a red-haired orphan who goes to live on a farm in Prince Edward Island.

Human Locomotion

1. It was such a nice day that we decided to stroll in the park.

2. My nephew is learning to walk. It's so funny to watch him toddle across the living-room.

3. The soldiers marched on to the parade grounds.

4. After work, I like to put on my running gear and go jogging in the park.

5. I got lost in that neighbourhood and I wandered around for a long time before I recognized some landmarks.

6. Let's go out to the countryside this weekend. We can go hiking in the hills.

7. After a full day of shopping, I trudged home exhausted.

8. I saw the bus coming, so I had to dash across the road to get to the stop on time.

9. The little girls were playing. They skipped down the street hand in hand.

10. In dance class, I learned to glide across the floor gracefully.

Going to the Cottage

1. **Winterize** means to make something suitable for use in the winter.

2. A **wimp** is a weak person who cannot get things done, and who is afraid of many things.

Glossary

Words are defined according to the way they are used in the text. Page references are in parentheses.

A

above grade level (10): beyond what is expected of a student at that level

academically (10): related to school and formal education

accelerator (68): the part of the car that makes it go faster, that gives the engine gas

access code (30): secret number used to make a transaction with a bank card

accommodations (60): place to sleep, live

account (30): a sum of money kept in a bank which may be added to and taken from

accurately (44): without making a mistake

ace up your sleeve (29): a good plan held back and produced if needed

addictive (27): causing a habit

adjective (19): a word that describes a noun

afford (27): to be able to buy

afraid (19, 41, 42): full of fear

air (70): to broadcast, to make known to others

airsick (56): feeling ill because of the motion of the plane

aisles (34): spaces between shelves or rows of seats, where people can walk

annual report (15, 16): a report on how well a company is doing, published once a year

appeal (34): to please, attract, interest

aquatics (18): sports happening in and around water

aroma (34): smell, usually pleasant

artificial (27): man-made, not natural

at least (2): in any case

auction (23): sale where customers offer money for objects, with the sale going to the highest bidder

B

baby teeth (34): teeth that young children have; they fall out and are replaced by permanent teeth

bachelor's degree (2): first rank in university, usually requiring three or four years of study

backache (42): pain in the back

bargain (23): try to make the price lower

battery (68): the part of the car that holds the electrical charge to start the engine

bed and breakfast (72, 73): home that offers tourists accommodations with breakfast included in the price, usually with shared bathroom facilities

beef (70): complaint (slang)

belly up (39, 40): dead (like a fish), usually used to describe bankrupt companies (slang)

bet (29): to risk money on the results of a future event

bid (23): to offer to pay a certain price at an auction or sale

bike path (22): pathway, often through park land, that is for cyclists and pedestrians

billboard (66): large, outdoor sign

bingo (29): a word called out when someone has won the game; an expression meaning someone has finished something or figured something out

biodegradable (57): breaking down naturally

black ice (71): ice that is the same colour as the asphalt on the road making it difficult to see

block (66): distance along a street from one cross street to another

boost (68): give power to the battery from another car

bother (33): to cause someone trouble, to make someone annoyed

boulevard (67): a wide street

braces (34): metal wires attached to teeth to correct their position

brake (68): the part of the car that makes it slow down and stop

braking distance (71): distance needed between cars to safely stop

branch (30): a local office

brand name (35): name given a product by a company

brand-new (23): not used

breakaway (20): a situation in which a player on one team gets past the defensive players to move towards the goal

bring up (6): mention

bring up children (6): raise children

broad-minded (22): accepting new and different ideas

brochure (4, 18): small, thin booklet (or folded paper) giving information

buck (23, 24): dollar (slang)

bug (41, 42): illness (informal)

bug (53, 54): to bother, annoy (slang)

by myself (16): alone, without help

by-law (42): law that is made by a local government or institution

C

calendar (3): a schedule and list of important dates including course information

call into the office (49): ask an employee to come to talk to the supervisor, usually for disciplinary reasons

camp (74): summer home

campus (66): school area with several buildings

can (49): fire, dismiss (slang)

can't stand (70): can't tolerate, don't like

cancellation (33): the act of calling off an appointment

cap (34): a covering for the top of something

cards on the table (29): everything out in the open, revealed

caretaker (49): janitor, someone who cleans and takes care of a building

carsick (56): feeling ill because of the motion of the car

catch a bug (41): get sick

cavity (34): a hole in a tooth

certificate (2): official paper showing that someone has finished a special course or program

chauffeur (19): a person employed to drive someone's car

check in (17): to report your arrival officially

check out (17): to have the removal of something officially noted

check out (33): to look at, examine

check-up (34): a general medical examination

checkout (34): where you pay for your purchases

chill (42): a feeling of cold in the body

chores (57): jobs, work

circulate (17): to move or flow, used for the practice of borrowing library books

circulation desk (16): desk in the library where you take your books to borrow or return them

circulation period (17): amount of time libraries books are allowed to be borrowed

clothes (57): things you wear

clustered (27): grouped together

cluttered (57): messy, with many things all around

cocoon (52): a protective home

cocooning (52): staying at home

cold (42): an illness marked by sneezing and coughing

cold turkey (43): quitting something suddenly

colloquial (7): conversational speech, everyday spoken language

come in handy (23, 39, 40): to be useful for something

come up with (6): think of something, produce a plan

commercial (27): related to business

commute (60): travel to another city to work

commuter (70): someone who travels to another city to work

compatible (59): suitable, comfortable together

computer literate (46): able to use computers

condo (56): condominium (shortened form), an apartment or townhouse that is bought, not rented

conference (39): a meeting of professionals with speeches and seminars

consultant (39): someone who gives professional advice to a company or individual

contagious (41): easily caught, used to describe diseases

controversial (27, 42): likely to cause or causing argument or disagreement

convenience food (52): prepared foods

conversational (7): everyday spoken language

cope (8): to deal successfully with something

cottage (74): summer home

cough (42): to clear something from the throat or lungs by pushing air out of the mouth

counsellor (3): a professional person who gives advice

court (67): a short one-way street, usually wide at the other end so that cars can turn around

craving (32): a desire for a particular food

crawl (71): to move very slowly, (literally) on hands and knees

crescent (67): a street that turns in a curve to join another street

crown (34): the part of the tooth that can be seen; an artificial piece to replace that part of the tooth

current releases (54): movies that are new, that are showing in the theatres

cut corners (72): to eliminate something to save time or money

cut down on (24): reduce

cut someone off (70): to go in front of someone, interfering with their path

D

daily (21): daily newspaper

dark (53): not light

dash (72, 73): run quickly across

databases (46): computer programs where information is stored and sorted

daydream (28): imagine something nice that could happen in the future

dead end (67): a street with no other exit

deaf (59): not able to hear

decay (34): to go bad, to be damaged

deep-fry (32): cook food immersed in oil

degree (2): a rank or title given by a university to a person who has successful completed a program of study

deke (20): a fake offensive move that is designed to take the defender out of position (Canadian, informal)

den (60, 61): small, quiet room in a house

dental hygienist (34): a person who cleans and treats people's teeth

deposit (30): to put money in the bank

desktop publishing (46): producing printed documents with the aid of a computer

diploma (2): official paper showing that someone has finished a program in school

directory (15): a book or list of names or facts, arranged in alphabetical order

dismiss (49): fire from a job, take someone's job away

distract (36): to take a person's mind off something else

distribute (6): to give out something to many people

doctorate (2): third rank in university, usually requiring three to seven years of study after a master's degree; also called Ph.D.

document (3): official paper that gives information or proof of something

domestic (57): related to the home

doubles as (61): serves another function

down-sized (49): reduced, made smaller

draft (48): first version of a document

draw (27): the act of picking a winning ticket or number

drifting snow (71): snow that is blown across the ground by the wind

drill (34): tool used to make holes

drive (67): a curving street with park land around it

drop out (8, 27): to stop attending or taking part

drop-in centre (27): an informal place for young people to come to for help or recreation

drop-off point (70): a place to leave travellers

dump (24): a place where garbage is placed

dying (72): wanting something very much (slang)

E

e-mail (48, 54): electronic mail, message sent over computer network

earache (42): pain in the ear

eat up (6): eat everything

edit (48): to prepare a document for publication by making corrections and eliminating unnecessary sections

efficiently (44): working well and without waste

electronic (46): anything related to products such as radios, televisions, computers

elementary school (2): first six to eight years of school

ellipsis (43): leaving something out to make a short form

en suite bathrooms (60): bathrooms joined to a bedroom

enthusiastically (44): with a strong interest in something

etiquette (62): rules for polite behaviour

evaluate (3, 4): to judge the value or level of something

every now and then (27): once in a while, occasionally

exact fare (70): the correct price of a ticket, with no change given

extension (13): more time to complete an assignment

F

far-sighted (22): thinking about the future

fare (70): cost of transportation

fast food (31): inexpensive food like hamburgers and pizza that is easily available and made quickly

fax (47): facsimile, a picture of a document sent over the phone lines

fear (19): to be afraid of

feedback (35): response, information

fender bender (72): a slight accident with damage to the car but no injury to people

fever (41): high body temperature, an indication of illness

fibre (31): plant matter that is not digested by the body but is needed to provide bulk in the digestive system

figure (8, 28): think

figures (46): I'm not surprised (informal expression)

file (33): a collection of paper or records on a certain subject, kept together

fill in (3): to complete a form by writing the information asked for fill out (3): to complete a form by writing the information asked for

filling (34): something used to fill holes in teeth

fine (18): penalty, money charged for breaking a rule or being late

finish a basement (55, 56): to put rooms in a basement

fire (49): to dismiss someone from a job

fish 'n chips (32): a dish of fish fried in batter and french fries

fit in (46): to suit, to find a place

flea market (23): place where small second-hand goods are sold

flu (42): influenza, a virus disease like a cold but more severe

fluoride treatment (34): putting a chemical (fluoride) on the teeth to prevent cavities

fonts (46): different styles of print

food court (31): a place with a number of small restaurants and a common eating area

for ages (33): for a long time

free (33): with no other engagements

freelancer (39): a trained worker who sells his or her work without being part of a company, e.g. most writers

freezing (34): using a local anaesthetic to numb sensation, to make part of the body unable to feel pain

French immersion (55, 56): form of schooling where English-speaking children study in French

fright (19): the feeling or experience of fear

frighten (19): to make afraid

from the sidelines (10): watching, not participating, in an activity (often used for sports)

G

gadget (46): a small instrument or tool

geez (8): expression of surprise

generic (35): shared by others, a characteristic

generic name (35): a name of a kind of thing, not a brand name

germs (42): very small things that cause illness

get around to something (23, 33): to find time to do something

get canned (49): to get fired from a job (slang)

get over (18): to find a way to deal with something

get sacked (49): to get fired from a job (slang)

get the hang of something (30): to learn how to do something and get comfortable doing it

get the night off (53): to have time off, to not have to work

get used to (8): to become accustomed to something

give out (6): to distribute, deliver

give something a shot (31): to try to do something

glide (73): to move smoothly

gonna (8, 20, 39, 43): going to (informal, spoken short form)

graphics (46): artwork, pictures, designs

grind (68): the noise of metal rubbing against other metal

guys (57): men, boys, people (slang)

H

handout (9): pages of information distributed in class

hang (30): to fix something so the lower part is free

hang a left (30): make a left turn

hang a right (30, 66): make a right turn

hang around (30): spend time someplace (informal)

hang around with (30): keep company with

hang on (27, 30): wait (informal)

hang out (27): to live, stay (slang)

hang up (30): to put something on a hook or hanger

hang-out (30): a place to stay (informal)

hardware (46): computer equipment

have a seat (10): sit down (informal)

have got (23): have, own (informal)

hazard (70): danger

head in the clouds (28): not thinking about real life, daydreaming

headache (42): pain in the head

heavy (53): needs definition

help oneself (60, 61): serve oneself to food that is offered

high tech (16): high technology (informal, shortened form), used to refer to the latest in electronic instruments

hike (73): to go for a long walk for exercise, usually in the countryside

historical site (72): place of historical significance

hit the ignition (68): start the car engine with the key

hit the jackpot (30): win a prize, get lucky

homesick (54, 56): longing to be home, missing home

homey (35): like home, comfortable

households (52): people who live in a house or apartment

housework (57): household chores like cleaning and doing the dishes

humane (60): showing human kindness and the qualities of a civilized position

humane society (60): place that takes in abandoned pets

I

immoral (27): not considered good or right

immunization (3): making the body safe from disease by injecting a medicine

impulse (34): a sudden wish to do something

in no time (32): soon, quickly

in-house (39): within the company or organization

incinerator (24): a furnace where garbage is burned

inconvenient (12, 13): not convenient, not suitable

indifferently (44): without caring about what happens

industriously (44): working very hard

influenza (42): flu, a virus disease like a cold but more severe

informal (7): casual, relaxed, not according to formal rules

injection (3): putting something into the body with a needle

interactive (48): with two-way communication, requiring the user's participation

Internet (48, 54): a network of computers all around the world

itinerary (72): planned route, schedule for a trip

J

jackpot (30): the biggest amount of money to be won in a game

janitor (49): cleaner, maintenance person for a building

jargon (48): words and phrases used by a particular group or profession

jog (73): to run for exercise, not too quickly

junk food (31): food that has little nutritional value

K

keep the books (54, 56): to keep track of payments, make financial records for a company

keyboarding (46): typing on a computer keyboard

kid (8, 55): child (informal)

kinda (33, 56): kind of (informal spoken form)

kindergarten (2): first year of school for children aged 4-5, often half-day and optional, preparation for Grade 1

L

landfill (24): place where garbage is buried

landmark (67): building, structure or physical feature that is easy to see

landscaping (39): action of making land around a building more interesting by planting trees and flowers

laryngitis (42): illness where one is unable to talk

lay off (39, 49): to take away someone's job because of changes in the company, usually because of financial problems, supposed to be a temporary job loss

layout (46, 55, 56): arrangement

league (19): a group of sports clubs that play games against each other

legally blind (46): with very little sight

let go (49): be taken off the staff

light (53): easy to understand

likely (34): probable, expected to happen

line-up (31): people waiting their turn in a line

lion's share (57): the most part

liquidate stock (39, 40): sell stock for cash

loan (30): money that is borrowed

loiter (27): to wander about or stay in a place without purpose

long-winded (22): talking a lot

look forward to (56): to anticipate, to want to happen

look into (6): to examine the meaning or causes of something

look something over (3): to examine, often to make a quick evaluation

look through something (4): to examine, especially for points to notice

LRTs (70): Light Rail Transit trains

lure (27): to attract, to tempt

M

madhouse (53): place where everyone is acting crazy

maintenance worker (49): someone who maintains equipment or a building

make a deal (24): to come to an agreement about a sale

make an appointment (34): to arrange to meet someone

make oneself at home (60, 61): to act as if one is at home

make-up test (12): supplemental test written when the regularly scheduled test is missed

march (73): to walk with a regular, forceful step like a soldier

Maritimes (72, 73): Nova Scotia, New Brunswick, and Prince Edward Island

master's degree (2): second rank in university, usually requiring one to three years after bachelor's level

mean to (33): intend to

memo (47): business correspondence within a company

menu (16): list of choices available, used for restaurants and computers

merit (49): deserving something

methodically (44): following a method, a planned way of doing things

midterm (12): halfway during a school term or semester

mind (58): to object to, dislike

molar (34): large back tooth used for grinding food

mongrel (60): mixed-breed dog

moving sale (23): special sale held to reduce stock before a move

muffler (68): the part of the car that makes the engine less noisy

municipal council (22): elected officials who govern the city

mutt (60): mongrel, mixed-breed dog (slang)

N

narrow-minded (22): not accepting new and different ideas

nausea (41, 42): feeling of sickness and a desire to vomit

near-sighted (22): not being able to see things far away

needle (3): a very thin hollow pointed tube that is used to put medicine or drugs into the body

night owl (59): someone who likes to stay up late at night (idiom)

ninja (53): martial arts expert

no good (43): it can't be done (expression)

no problem (66): you're welcome (slang expression)

noun (19): a word that is the name of a person, place, or thing

nursery (39, 40): place where plants are grown before they are planted in the ground permanently

nutritional (31): providing value from food

O

on hold (48): waiting for someone on the phone

on one's game (20): playing well

on the air (70): broadcasting on radio or television

on time (10): not late, happening at the expected time, punctual

on-line (54): using your computer to communicate with other computers over phone lines or other connections

open house (10, 11): informal social event open to all who wish to come, an occasion when institutions such as schools and factories are open to the public

or so (4): approximately

outgrow (23): get too big or old for something

outhouse (74): toilet in a shed outside the main building

outlet (31): a store selling the products of a certain business

outside line (48): a telephone line that connects to the outside, not an internal line

overcome (18): to fight successfully

overhead projector (9): machine that shows on a screen what is written on a transparent sheet

P

packaged (34): in some kind of container or bag

pamphlet (2): a small book with paper covers that usually deals with official information, sometimes just a folded sheet of paper

parental leave (52): leave from work to take care of a baby

particles (5): short words like prepositions and articles that are not as important as the main words

passes (70): a card that shows that one is able to travel without paying each time

performance (49): the action of doing something, what one has accomplished in a job

phrasal verb (5): verb that is more than one word

phrase (5): several words that go together

pink slip (39, 40, 49): a notice given to an employee to inform him he no longer has a job (slang)

placement test (3, 4): test given to find out a student's level, to place the student in a class

point-form (44): not in full sentences

pothole (71): hole in the pavement

prerequisite (3): course needed before another course can be taken

pretty (53): quite, rather

pricing (34): assigning cost to something

profession (2): an occupation requiring special education and training, especially law, medicine, and teaching

program (46): set of instructions which tells a computer what to do

promptly (44): on time, not late

protein (31): substances in foods (like meat and eggs) which help build up the body

pull a tooth (34): to take out a tooth

pull-out sofa (61): sofa that converts to a bed

purebred (60): descended from one breed or kind with no mixture of other breeds

put down (6): to record, enter

put off (33): to delay

put someone on hold (47): to make someone wait on the telephone

put someone up (61): to give someone a place to sleep

psych (8): psychology (shortened form)

R

re- (22): again (prefix)

realist (28): someone who accepts reality, the way things are

rec (18): recreation (informal, shortened form)

recycle (23): to use again

refinish (56): to put new paint or varnish on a piece of furniture

register (2, 4): to sign up for a course, to put one's name in an official list of students

registered trademark (35): a name that is licensed to that company

registration (4): process where students sign up for courses

reluctant to (52): not wanting to

resident (16): someone who lives in a particular place

retail (23, 27): the business of selling things directly to the consumer

rethink (22): think again

right around the corner (60): close by (idiom)

roommate (59): someone unrelated who shares a room, apartment, or house

rotary dial (47): the wheel on the telephone with holes for each number

route (70): the way the bus goes from one stop to another

rubbernecking (71): looking at an accident as you pass on the road

rummage sale (23): sale of donated second-hand items

run off (72): to escape

run out of time (10): to have no more time left

S

salaried workers (41): workers that have an annual rate of pay (a salary) rather than workers that have an hourly rate of pay (a wage)

save (20): to stop a goal

scare (19): to make someone feel fear

scary (19): causing fear

school board (2): a group of people, usually elected, who manage the schools in an area, also called a board of education

schooling (2): education

scrap (22): abandon, discard, throw away

scratch-and-win (27): a ticket where the player scratches off a substance covering the game board

screen (60): to examine to prove the suitability of something or someone

screw something up (31): to do something wrong

sec (27): second (shortened form, informal)

second-hand (23): used, not new

secondary school (2): school for teenaged children, after elementary school and before college or university (also called high school)

see someone off (70): to say good-bye to a traveller

seeing-eye dog (59): a dog used to help blind people get around

sense of humour (46): an ability to laugh about things

settle in (10): to make yourself comfortable in a new situation, get used to something

short cut (66): shorter, quicker way to get somewhere

short notice (61): not much time before the event

short-handed (22): needing help or staff

short-lived (22): not lasting a long time

short-sighted (22): not thinking about the future

short-tempered (22): easily angered

shorthand (9): special writing using abbreviations and symbols, used by secretaries to take dictation

shot (2, 3): injection, needle

sick leave (41): time taken off work because of illness

sick to one's stomach (42): vomiting or feeling like one wants to

sign up (3, 54): to register, enroll, put one's name in for something like a course skid (72): to slip sideways on a road

skip (73): to move in a light, dancing way

slam (72): to hit hard

slam on the brakes (72): to hit the brake pedal hard and suddenly

slang (7): language that is not acceptable in formal situations, language regarded as very informal or not polite

sleep-over (60): staying overnight

sloppily (44): taking little care to do something right

smoke detector (59): an instrument that sounds an alarm when there is a fire in the building

smoke-free (42): not allowing smoking in the area

sneeze (42): to clear the nose with a violent, sudden pushing of air

snug (52): secure, tight

sofa bed (60, 61): sofa that contains a mattress for sleeping

software (46): instructions for a computer

soothing (46): calming, relaxing

sore throat (42): pain in the throat making it difficult to swallow or talk

spring clean (23, 24): thorough annual cleaning

squash (61): game played in a four-walled court with racquets and a soft rubber ball

stable (52): not changing, dependable

staff (49): employees, people working for a company

stands (20): a raised place where people can sit or stand to watch sports events

start-up costs (39, 40): costs associated with starting a business

stir-fry (32): to cook food (cut in small pieces) quickly in a small amount of oil and stirring it often

stomach-ache (42): pain in the stomach

strategy (9): a plan for doing something

streetcar (70): bus that goes along tracks in the roadway

stride (27): to walk with long steps

stroll (73): to walk slowly for pleasure

suit (4): to fit, be convenient

supposed to (62): expected to

surplus (23): extra, not needed

sympathetic (41): feeling sorry for someone

symptom (42): a sign of an illness

T

T.A. (8): Teaching Assistant

tailgate (70): to follow another car too closely

take turns (53): to share something, with each person getting a chance to do something

take-out food (52): food from a restaurant that you take home to eat

tear up (6): to rip into little pieces

teleconferencing (47): having a meeting over the phone lines instead of in person

teller (30): person who makes bank transactions

terrify (19): to make someone feel great fear

terror (19): a very great fear

there's no way (43): it's impossible (informal expression)

throw up (42): to vomit, to bring up the contents of the stomach and out through the mouth

ticked off (20): angry (slang)

ticket (70): piece of card or paper giving letting someone enter somewhere

toddle (73): to walk unsteadily, like a small child

token (70): a piece of plastic or metal that represents something like a ticket

toothache (34, 42): pain in a tooth

touch tone (47): phone with buttons instead of a dial

tough (39): hard, difficult

traffic jam (71): cars blocked together on the road

transfer (47): to move the call to another phone line

transfer (70): a piece of paper allowing one to move from one bus to another

transfer funds (30): move money from one account to another

trudge (73): to walk with heavy steps, slowly and with effort

tuition (3): fees for a school year or semester

turn (an age) (2): have a birthday and become a year older

turn on (6, 21): to make something work by using a switch

turnstile (70): a small gate with four arms that spin around as someone passes through

typing (46): tapping keys on a machine to produce writing

U

uneasy (10): anxious, worried, troubled

uninhabited (65): not lived in

used to (9, 18): be accustomed to

V

vaccination (3): making the body safe from disease by injecting a medicine

veg (53): vegetate (shortened form, slang)

veg out (53): lie around doing nothing (slang)

vegetate (53): lie around not doing much (slang)

verb (19): a word or phrase that tells what someone or something is, does, or experiences

vitamin (31): chemicals found in foods which are needed by the body for health

voice mail (47): system of recorded messages allowing the caller to leave a message

voice recognition system (46): a computer's ability to process the human voice

vomit (43): to throw up the contents of the stomach through the mouth

W

wander (73): to walk aimlessly, without purpose

wanna (56): want to (informal, shortened spoken form)

wear out a welcome (56, 57): stay too long so that your hosts want you to leave

weave (70): to move in and out

web site (48): a place where you can get information on the Internet

what say (72): let's (expression used to make a suggestion)

whew (8): I'm glad that's over! (expression)

whim (49): a sudden idea or wish, often unreasonable

whimsical (49): with strange ideas

whimsy (49): strange act or idea

whine (68): make a sharp, high, irritating noise

whoa (23): stop! (informal expression of surprise)

whole bit (41): everything

wimp (74): a weak person

windshield (68): the glass at the front of the car

winterize (74): to prepare for winter

wisdom tooth (34): one of the four large back teeth that usually do not appear until adulthood

wish list (63): things that one would like to have

withdrawal (30): taking money out of a bank account

word processing (46): using a computer to write documents

workplace (39): the world of work, the place where one works

workshop (39): a class or seminar on a specific skill, usually with hands-on practice

World Wide Web (48): a network of information joined by "hypertext links" so that you can go from one piece of information to another, even though the documents are stored on different computers

Y

yard sale (23): sale of personal items

yellowish (66): an off-shade of yellow

Z

zip (70): move quickly sideways

zoo (8): a wild place (slang)